A Year on Ice

Living and Working in Antarctica

A YEAR ON ICE

LIVING AND WORKING IN ANTARCTICA

WARREN HERRICK

SHOAL BAY PRESS

DEDICATION

To Scotty
Who in his own words ...
'Spat the dummy and shot the gap,
but no drama, carry on!'
and
To the rest of the Scott Base 1994-95 winter-over team:
Bruce, Dave, Jan, Jim, Joe, John, Sean and Tom.

First published in 1997 by
Shoal Bay Press Ltd
Box 2151, Christchurch, New Zealand

Copyright © 1997 Warren Herrick

ISBN 0 908704 56 9

Printed in Hong Kong through Bookprint Consultants Ltd, Wellington

CONTENTS

ACKNOWLEDGMENTS

Thanks first and foremost to Liz, whose selflessness not only accommodated my three visits to Antarctica, with the first occasion only three months after our marriage, but hours, days, weeks and months of book typing, retyping and perusing photos.

Thanks are also due to the following:

David Harrowfield, the perfect mentor and entertaining host during my numerous visits to Christchurch.

Liz, David and Tim Higham, who offered advice and checked the manuscript.

Those named contributors (to each chapter) whose inspired writing adds a further dimension to this work, and Margaret Bradshaw who provided material for Trevor Hatherton's obituary.

Colin Monteath for his foreword and Mark Pickering for drafting the book's maps.

The Shoal Bay Press team: David, Ros, Rachel, Luke and Jill.

The 'Big Bananas' literary fund.

Numerous others include: many Antarctica New Zealand (formerly NZAP) staff, Pedro Nelson, Nigel Roberts and Buzz Burrows; Robbie Burton, whose comments put the book on the right track; friends Geoff Spearpoint and Barb Brown at Birdlings Flat for their encouragement while we stayed next door at Mark's bach. Birdlings, with its wonderful sunsets, was an inspirational location for creating an initial draft of a manuscript.

Antarctic, the quarterly publication of the Antarctic Society, was an invaluable source of information.

Grateful thanks to the publishers for short extracts from the following sources: A.S. Helm & J.H. Miller's *Antarctica,* R.E. Owen, Government Printer, Wellington, 1964 (p.39); Adrian Hayter's *The Year of the Quiet Sun,* Hodder & Stoughton Ltd, 1968 (p.59); Richard Bach's *Illusions – The Adventures of a Reluctant Messiah,* William Heinemann Ltd, 1977 (p.73); Nigel Gifford's *Expeditions & Exploration,* MacMillan London Ltd, 1983 (p.77); Apsley Cherry-Garrard's *The Worst Journey in the World,* Chatto & Windus London Ltd, 1937 (p.102).

FOREWORD

Before my departure for Antarctica in 1973 I pored through Adrian Hayter's book *The Year of the Quiet Sun* for information about life at Scott Base. Even then, in the early 1970s, both the base and the structure of the New Zealand Antarctic programme had been superseded by events since Hayter's year on Ross Island almost a decade before.

Now, 30 years on, it is high time to record a fresh look at the experience of working in this harsh and remote polar environment. The last 20 years have seen near-continual change to the scope and nature of New Zealand's scientific endeavour in Antarctica, in part brought on after the complete rebuilding of Scott Base during the 1980s.

While it is remarkable that no one has created this record of the essence of Scott Base in the past three decades, especially relating to the unique winter-over experience, it has been worth waiting for Warren Herrick's story.

A Year on Ice provides a window into life on an Antarctic base, and Warren's open, frank style allows a personal insight into the nine men and one woman who staffed the base in the winter of 1995, together with their routines, pranks, traditions and, inevitably, their conflicts.

Warren's chapters are interspersed with short accounts by past Scott Base 'winter-overers', who describe aspects of their own experiences: filming emperor penguins in winter at Cape Crozier, saying farewell to the huskies, an emergency midwinter medi-vac, and apple-pieing Prime Minister Robert Muldoon.

A Year on Ice, released to coincide with the 40th anniversary of the opening of Scott Base, makes it clear that New Zealand continues to make a valuable contribution to modern polar science. New Zealand also plays a pivotal role in its stewardship of the continent by initiating and implementing practical, effective environmental management procedures. Long may this continue.

This fine book is a worthy successor to *The Year of the Quiet Sun*. It will be of interest to anyone with a yen to know more about life in the white wilderness perched on our southern doorstep.

Colin Monteath
Hedgehog House

INTRODUCTION

E very February the nation's newspapers carry a situations vacant advertisement that instils feelings of excitement and hope in many New Zealanders. On offer is a unique 'paid' wilderness-type experience: the chance to be part of a select team required to staff Scott Base, situated in one of the world's most beautiful and challenging locations. Unfortunately many aspirants are disappointed. The lucky few are selected to experience either a period of up to four months during the austral summer as summer staff, or to join the *crème de la crème*, remaining for a whole year as members of the small winter-over team.

Virtually every Antarctic text acquaints the reader with the continent as the coldest, windiest and driest place on earth. However, for the 'winter-overer' these elements become overshadowed by the impact of night being day during summer, and day being night during winter. Moving between these seasons, with their accompanying glorious displays of colour, is an unforgettable pleasure.

Yet few texts establish the exact nature of this mysterious cycle of day and night in Antarctica, which varies according to latitude. Scott Base, at 77°51'S, follows a bimonthly cycle, with the 21st day of each second month (approximately) marking the changes.

The year's final sunset occurs on 21 October and the sun remains above the horizon for the next four months. 21 December marks the austral midsummer, with the sun at its highest for the entire 24 hours. The sun first sets again on 21 February, when most of the summer staff are back home.

Close to 21 April, when the sun rises and sets for the last time before the four months of winter, the occasion is celebrated with a sunset dinner. From then, with the sun below the horizon for the entire 24 hours, the days get shorter then darker until austral midwinter on 21 June when the sun is at its lowest (below the horizon). The sun first rises again on 21 August.

Although the sun disappears for four months, it is not entirely dark during this time. Day-long darkness lasts only about six weeks – for three weeks either side of midwinter's day.

Technically, in terms of latitude, Scott Base is not in darkness all 24 hours of the shortest day. For a short period near midday the sun rises to between 12-18° below the horizon, which gives a measure of astronomical twilight, the darkest of three levels. (Civil twilight occurs at 0-6° below and nautical twilight occurs at 6-12° below.) However, because Scott Base is on the southern side of Ross Island, whose peaks obscure northern horizons, these six weeks are essentially continuously dark.

During the year, life at Scott Base follows normal day-in, day-out routines. A 'night on the town' (at McMurdo) in broad daylight during summer and a day at work during winter's darkness defy the usual definitions. It can take a bit of getting used to.

A Year on Ice is an attempt to broach a literary void, describing 'warts and all' life during a year's living and working at Scott Base. This 1994-95 snapshot focuses on the events and life of only one of 40 winter-over teams (listed in Appendix 5) but also portrays the experience of other years.

It is written for those who have experienced Scott Base, for those aspirants who have never had the luck on their side, and for those for whom this book will sow the seed of an Antarctic experience: *A Year on Ice* is written to evoke memories and provoke dreams.

Warren Herrick

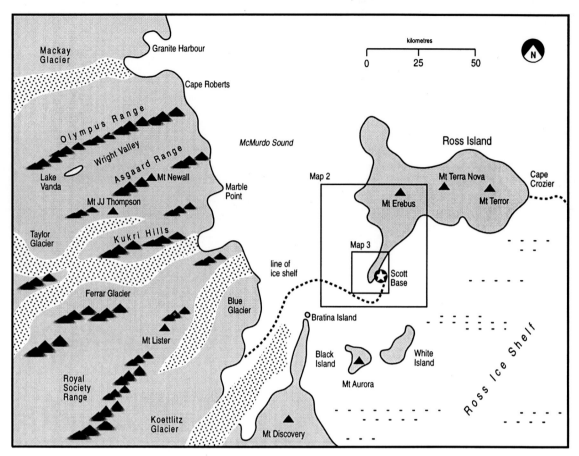

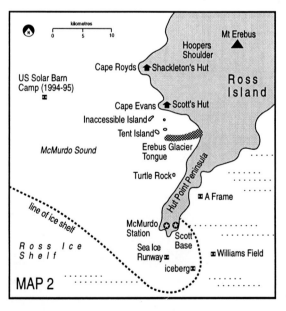

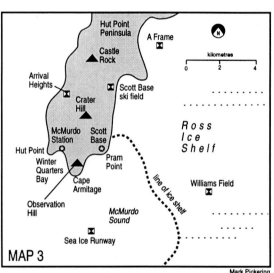

The Ross Island region of Antarctica

Mark Pickering

1

SCOTT BASE

S cott Base is New Zealand's southernmost installation. Its location at Pram Point, on the tip of Ross Island's Hut Point Peninsula, is at a latitude of 77°51'S – 3832km south of Christchurch and 1353km from the South Pole, according to the Automobile Association sign in front of the base. This neat collection of light green buildings supports New Zealand's national Antarctic science programme and is home to annual winter-over teams.

Robert Falcon Scott named Pram Point during the 1901-04 Discovery expedition. Scott's team had to use a small boat (pram) to cross the open water of McMurdo Sound to get to the Ross Ice Shelf

Scott Base on a perfect morning in March

late in summer. This permanent floating sheet of ice covers part of the Ross Sea, extending for hundreds of kilometres east and south of Ross Island. When the sea in McMurdo Sound freezes it almost merges continuously with this shelf.

Scott Base enjoys a panoramic outlook. A convenient due-north reference point fixes on Mt Erebus (3795m), Ross Island's highest point and an active volcano. A clockwise sweep of the skyline passes the summits of Mt Terra Nova (2130m) and Mt Terror (3230m), then Ross Island falls away to a flat eastern horizon over the Ross Ice Shelf. A fix on the South Pole can be made through the gap between snow-clad White Island and snow-free Black Island, both piercing the shelf's ice. Antarctica's mainland fills the west, with rounded Mt Discovery (2680m) dominating the south-west corner and the majestic Royal Society Range, over 100km away, sweeping up the western limits of McMurdo Sound. This range disappears from view behind local high points Observation Hill and Crater Hill.

The United States programme's McMurdo Station is only 3km from Scott Base, beyond Observation Hill and overlooking Winter Quarters Bay. During the winters of 1902 and 1903 Scott's party were the first to winter over on Ross Island, living aboard their ship *Discovery*, which had become locked in the frozen waters of this bay. The Discovery expedition's hut still stands at Hut Point and contrasts dramatically with the modern metropolis of McMurdo.

In May 1955 the New Zealand government announced it would support Briton Dr Vivian Fuchs's proposed Trans-Antarctic Expedition (TAE) of 1957–58. Fuchs's party became the first to cross the continent, travelling from the Weddell Sea to the Ross Sea via the South Pole.

Edmund Hillary led the Kiwi TAE contingent. During the summer of 1956–57 they sailed south on the HMNZS *Endeavour*, selected Pram Point as a site and began building Scott Base. On 20 January

Ramon Tito (extreme left) raises New Zealand's flag, 20 January 1957

RAMON'S STORY

We set sail for McMurdo Sound from Bluff on 21 December 1956, under the command of Captain Harry Kirkwood, Royal Navy. On board was a crew of 15, plus the expedition party.

The first days at sea were uneventful but it was definitely becoming cooler. As most of the ship's company hadn't experienced snow and ice before, some were apprehensive when we sighted our first iceberg. As we neared the Ross Sea the little bits of floating ice became bigger, then a little larger, and then we had to sail around them. Awesome! It's amazing to think that four-fifths of the berg is underwater.

Then came the ice pack – another milestone on our journey south. We became ice-bound at one stage so went ashore the pack to kick around our football until things became a little precarious. The ice-breaker USS *Glacier* came to our rescue and punched a pathway through the ice. During this time we were introduced to some of the locals – little chaps dressed in black and white tuxedos. There was the occasional whale and seal and numerous skuas.

After what seemed like days in the pack ice we arrived in McMurdo Sound, secured to the ice and spent a day of orientation. Then, after unloading, preparations were made for erecting the first hut. For a while we thought it was not going to happen as the scoria ground was frozen solid with permafrost. But with good old Kiwi knowhow the day was soon won and everyone involved was very satisfied – another milestone.

It was announced that there would be an opening ceremony for Scott Base and our captain said to

Ramon Tito

me, 'Because you are the youngest on board the *Endeavour* we're giving you the privilege of raising the New Zealand flag.' Me!

When we arrived back in New Zealand I found the flag-raising had caused a bit of fuss, especially back in Taranaki in my home town of Waitara. My Te Atiawa and Taranaki-Turu people certainly made it known who I was and to whom I belonged. 'Local boy puts us on the map' sort of thing.

When I look back I do feel a sense of pride, firstly just being asked to raise the flag and secondly, how proud my people here at home felt for me. Now in 1996 when the family gathers, my wife Edith and sons Trevor and Trini still talk about my little exploit at Scott Base on 20 January 1957.

I couldn't have imagined wintering over. The ship was tentatively scheduled for a trip around the Pacific Islands; that sounded more like me.

[Ramon made three trips to Antarctica with the *Endeavour*, served out his time with the navy until 1962 and returned to Waitara to work for the Post Office/Telecom for 25 years. Since then he's worked with training and education schemes involving Maori youth. He has also been involved with iwi fishing and land issues.]

1957 Scott Base was officially opened during a simple ceremony in which 20-year-old Ramon Tito, the youngest member of the *Endeavour*'s crew, raised the New Zealand flag.

After the first winter at Scott Base Hillary's team drove modified Massey Ferguson farm tractors towards the Pole, laying fuel and supply depots for Fuchs. With the task complete at the last depot,

800km from the Pole, they made some calculations. They had enough fuel and time, so they shelved their original plan and pushed on, arriving at the South Pole 16 days ahead of Fuchs, who was experiencing heavier going on his Weddell Sea approach.

While Fuchs and Hillary were crossing the continent's open expanses, the world's science community was conducting another event in Antarctica on

A. Incinerator
B. Dangerous goods store
C. Fuel tanks
D. Vehicle hitching rail
E. Freezer (food)
F. Field store
G. Hangar
H. Light workshop complex

I. Heavy workshop
J. Pump shed
K. Administration area, shop
L. Powerhouse, RO plant
M. Wet lab
N. Storage area
0. Flagpole
P. Kitchen

Q. Dining area
R. Bar
S. Water tanks
T. Warm store (food)
U. Accommodation,
   ablutions, laundry
V. Sewerage outlet
W. TAE hut (museum)

X. Old base (since removed)
Y. Hatherton Laboratory
Z. Q Hut (summer accom-
   modation, laboratory,
   library, gymnasium)

a grander scale – the International Geophysical Year (IGY) of 1957-58. Five New Zealand scientists, led by Dr Trevor Hatherton, travelled to Scott Base to make our contribution to IGY.

The success of this event heralded the beginnings of a national research programme in the Ross Dependency, the segment of Antarctica New Zealand has administered since 1923. In May 1962 it was announced that Scott Base would remain as a permanent scientific installation.

The original Scott Base, which resembled a collection of orange/yellow oversized packing cases, became dated technologically and in the way it could fulfil other expectations. More than a paint job was required, so in 1974 the Ministry of Works and Development began planning its replacement with a new state-of-the-art construction.

Scott Base adopted its signatory 'RBT green' in 1967-68. The story goes that Bob Thomson (RBT), who headed New Zealand's programme during 1965-88, argued that since white crofters' cottages in the green fields of England were pleasing to the eye, the converse should equally apply.

Scott Base's reconstruction began during the summer of 1976-77 with the erection of Q Hut, a summer accommodation and laboratory building. Since the trial design of this building, subsequent construction has been much improved.

Each summer, over a period of a decade, the next step in a staged plan followed: the powerhouse in 1978-79, sleeping accommodation and ablution area in 1980-81, kitchen, mess (now known as dining area) and bar in 1981-83, the command centre (now known as administration) in 1983-84, the

Hatherton Laboratory in 1984-85, the light workshop complex in 1985-87 and the heavy workshop in 1986-88.

One 1957 building remains. The original kitchen and mess building has been relocated closer to the foreshore and preserved for posterity as the TAE hut. The hangar, constructed in 1959-60 to house Royal New Zealand Air Force aircraft flown in support of New Zealand's programme, is now used as a store.

The new base utilises cold-store construction technology. Foundations are frozen into place in the ground's permafrost and a steel skeleton framework supports large panels of cladding. These panels, two layers of sheet metal sandwiching a thick polyurethane foam filling, are very strong and they're locked together as roof, walls and under-floor. The complete seal formed provides maximum insulation and, inside this cavity, regular construction presents a homely finish, with wallpaper on the walls and vinyl or carpet on the floor in most buildings. Windows are all double or treble glazed, and the doors to the outside are like those found on walk-in freezer units.

Scott Base's buildings are connected by linkways, which afford much comfort when the weather deteriorates. As a fire precaution, fire doors in these linkways will automatically close and isolate any affected building. The under-floor cavity through the whole complex, including linkways, allows power, water and sewerage utilities to be kept warm.

Scott Base has three 180kV generators to produce the base's electricity. JP-8 grade fuel (aircraft turbine fuel with additives), shipped south by tanker late each summer, fires one generator at a time. Three are required for breakdown and fire scenarios, with two located in the main powerhouse and the third in an emergency powerhouse in the light workshop complex.

Heating is provided by reticulating hot water throughout the base. The water is heated in water jackets around the exhausts of the generators and supplementary oil-fired heaters assist to maintain a constant 20°C throughout the base.

About 1000 litres of fuel are needed daily for power, heat and water production.

The base's first reverse osmosis (RO) water plant, commissioned in the early 1980s, has ended the laborious task of collecting snow and ice to feed the ice melters. RO de-salinates seawater. The base's water plant can produce 6000 litres each day and up to 160,000 litres is stored in four storage tanks. This supply doubles as a firefighting reserve and, as water is not cheap to produce, conservation is encouraged.

Sewage is macerated and flushed into the sea in front of Scott Base. There's little problem if this sewage is taken up into the RO unit as fine RO membranes filter out most organic pathogenic nasties. Continued monitoring keeps a check on both the purity of RO-produced water and the effects sewage discharge is having on local marine life. Strict guidelines prohibit the flushing of chemicals and pollutants down the sink.

Environmental awareness has become one of Antarctica's more important issues during the 1990s.

Previous attempts to protect the continent centred on formulating rules to minimise any impact of mineral exploitation, an activity many nations believed to be inevitable.

Environmental groups, particularly Greenpeace, which operated its World Park base at Cape Evans on Ross Island during 1987-92, led the way towards a policy of absolute protection. Greenpeace campaigned to highlight the impact national programmes were already having on this pristine environment. This has positively assisted the shaping of more comprehensive protection, with the United Nations eventually voting to declare Antarctica a world park.

A home for a year

As a consequence, the Protocol on Environmental Protection to the Antarctic Treaty (also known as the Madrid Protocol) was signed in 1991 and ratified by New Zealand as the Antarctica (Environmental Protection) Act 1994. It binds all New Zealanders in Antarctica, whether working at Scott Base or working on any other national Antarctic programme, visiting as a tourist or taking part in a private expedition.

The main application of the Madrid Protocol for those in Antarctica is to the handling of waste. Scott Base's incineration of burnables (paper products, food scraps and food-contaminated plastics, medical waste and untreated timber) is presently under review and everything else, apart from the sewage pumped into the sea, is returned to New Zealand.

Science, rather than territory, has prospered as the main focus of international investment in Antarctica. It is for scientific purposes that New Zealand maintains Scott Base.

Scott Base becomes a hive of activity during summer, its population of science and support staff peaking at 60-70. When the last plane departs late in February, 10-12 winter-over staff remain. None of the base is closed down during winter and the increased space becomes very welcome, especially when winter's darkness confines most activities indoors.

On 4 October 1994 a year on ice began for 10 winter-over staff, selected by the New Zealand Antarctic Programme (NZAP) to support the 1994-95 year.

2
Building a Team

In pairs, as 'buddies', we grope our way around another lap of the Woolston Training Centre's breathing apparatus (BA) chamber – a darkened and heated maze of ramps, corners, ladders, holes and pipes. Our winter-over team are now into day six of an eight-day fire training course. After a number of runs through this obstacle course we're now memorising the layout.

'You! Right?' shouts Joe. His question, clipped and succinct, is understood even though talking through a BA facemask speech transmitter reduces most conversation to mumble.

'Yep!'

Joe Ford and I continue, taking care not to let our 'pineapple' (a fire hose coiled in pineapple shape) start unravelling. We also keep tabs on the life-line leading us through the maze, as well as always keeping in touch with our 'buddy'.

Any thoughts of Scott Base and its expansive white world are miles away while we are inside this place. The 24-hour-a-day daylight and cold temperatures that will greet us in October will be a total

contrast to this. This BA chamber emits a cacophony from a rumbling super-heater unit, demand valves issuing rushes of air into BA facemasks with each breath, reverberations from clambering hand and knee on the wooden planking, and muffled shouting through facemasks. Antarctica is silent.

New Zealand Fire Service training instructors Neill Price and Dave Berry survey our progress with brief flashes of torchlight. The darkness mimics the zero visibility of smoke and for safety reasons fire training is no longer conducted in real smoke. Neill promised we'd be worked hard and assistant Dave delivers.

'Come on, you guys!' snarls Dave, his voice clearly audible without BA. He has discerned some sluggishness.

Heavy black fire-retardant coats are very uncomfortable when you're sweaty and hot. But fully appreciating the importance of this training, we plod on with teeth gritted and dismiss any thoughts of revenge. Repetitive BA use breeds confidence – its positive pressure air delivery always keeps up with

Sweating it out in the BA chamber

Scott Base's complete 1994-95 fire crew

demand. The BA facemask rubber forms a good seal with facial skin. A new safety requirement this year requires all BA users to be clean shaven for training. Scotty (Shane Scott) and I have sacrificed beards for this.

The shrill of a whistle indicates that someone's tank pressure has dropped below 50 bars, which leaves them with only about 10 minutes' air. Is it Scotty? The larger or more unfit you are the greater your demand for air and Scotty has certainly been doing his fair share of 'sucking rust' (the taste of an empty tank). The alarm evokes a further rush of adrenalin for all, including Dave, who fixes his attention on the whistle.

Joe and I enjoy a timely escape, exiting into the day's light with our pineapple mostly intact. The large metal door of the chamber thumps closed on the commotion behind. Joe's pressure gauge registers 100 bars. Mine is down to 70. We head back to the BA room and cool off.

Fire is recognised as the greatest hazard at Scott Base. Any activity in Antarctica – the coldest, driest and windiest place on earth – can be serious business, so the prospect of containing a major fire there is daunting. This was impressed upon us during a session working in the blast freezers at the Belfast freezing works.

Eight days' preparation will not make an expert firefighter, but we are at least learning the fundamentals of, first, saving life, and second, containing fire. Fortnightly fire drills at Scott Base will keep us up to speed.

It's comforting to learn that Scott Base's electronic fire surveillance and reactionary facilities are second to none. McMurdo is large enough to have a professional firefighting crew and in the event of fire they would assist, weather permitting. Scott Base has never had a major fire and our fire crew motto is 'Our Aim, No Flame'.

Our first three days' fire training involve 14 Scott Base summer staff, who will assist with our fire crew duties during summer. The rest of the course our attention is undivided, providing the perfect opportunity to begin building a winter-over team.

But first, our summer companions are farewelled (for now) with dinner at the Kaiapoi Working Men's Club – Neill's club. The mood among other patrons

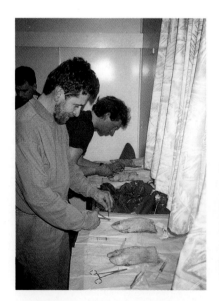

With Tarn Pilkington practising suturing technique with pigs' trotters.

Tarn and Rachel Brown assist during a ceremonial beard removal before fire training.

RAY LOGIE: 'THE FUEL DUMP'S ON FIRE!'

On 1 August 1961 Bernard Foley and Bill Hare were preparing to pump 2000 gallons of diesel fuel from a McMurdo tanker, drawn by a D8, into 44-gallon drums at the base's refuelling point.

A Herman Nelson heater, which was used to heat the fuel pump, caught fire. The fire spread to the big tractor and trailer and the fuel dump was only yards away.

At the time everyone was in the mess having a coffee. We grabbed dry-powder extinguishers and bolted. It was cold as hell (-44°F) and it almost ripped our lungs out. Luckily there was no wind.

The plume of black smoke rose hundreds of feet, with orange flames billowing. The American driver, brave man, was driving the burning tractor and trailer away from the dump.

As fire chief I gave only two orders: 'Get into it and go in low.' A twilight glow to the north of Erebus was providing enough light for the firefighters and a barrage of powder had it out in 10 minutes. Fortunately there were no injuries.

Fire training didn't really exist in the early days, and in our year we didn't even have any snowcraft instruction. Pre-Antarctic training in 1960 was at Wallis House in Lower Hutt in mid-September and Mr D. Dunnachie, the fire protection officer with the Ministry of Works, gave us a rundown on the base's fire amenities.

The month before our training eight scientists had perished in a fire at the Russian base, Mirny. It couldn't be contained as 126mph winds knocked the firefighters off their feet. At a temperature of -50°F the blizzard-borne snow crystals were sharp enough to cut them. The tracked vehicles with firefighting gear were practically immobilised in the cold and wind.

At Scott Base we did have firefighting drills, mainly using extinguishers to put out trays of burning diesel. We had no water for fighting fire, and relied on dry-powder, or carbon-dioxide extinguishers in the lab and radio room where there was delicate equipment. McMurdo would have come to help if we'd needed them.

Ray Logie

I tested the alarms every week and tested the extinguishers every three months. We had no smoke detectors and no breathing apparatus.

The following year the pre-Antarctic training was held at Waiouru, with snowcraft on Mt Ruapehu. Six men were given fire-prevention and firefighting instruction at the Fire Services Council's school at Island Bay in Wellington.

[Ray Logie wintered over at Scott Base in 1960-61 as the senior maintenance officer, had three days back in New Zealand, then returned to work as traverse engineer with the American Roosevelt Island Dome project during the summer of 1961–62. The Americans were happy to have a Kiwi mechanic on the project: polar transport expert Major Antero Havola told Ray that the Americans stopped producing mechanics when Henry Ford stopped making the Model T. Ray returned to Scott Base in summer 1962-63 as deputy leader.]

appears subdued in light of the day's by-election result. Kaiapoi, once a Labour Party stronghold, has been rezoned into the Selwyn electorate and the National Party has won. For us, the name of the club's Robert Falcon Scott bar with its display of Discovery expedition artefacts touches a stronger chord.

Back at Woolston on Monday morning, after a day off, we assemble with our commissioned BA sets. Neill alerts us to a fire behind the fire tower and, like sheep, all 10 of us don BA and run to it.

Caught. No team response. No one has taken control and no one has assessed the scene. No one has even thought about using the Wajax firefighting pump that we've spent most of Saturday learning about.

Neill isn't worried. He's seen all this before and dispatches us to 'suck rust' crawling on our hands and knees through water in the training centre's underground pipes.

The next 48 hours evidence almost complete redemption and a fire crew is gelling. Bruce Calder and Tom Hopkins are filling crew chief roles, with the rest slotting into positions of engineer/hose-layer, Wajax operator or BA-equipped firefighting pair. Two crews of five are required for the week-on/week-off roster during winter.

Winter team-building is also progressing well. There is genuine mutual interest and acceptance among us, indicating a high degree of tolerance and maturity that augur well for our year ahead.

Jan Stratford learned she'd be the only woman in our winter team when we first met at the training camp at Tekapo. It was immediately apparent that this was no problem for Jan, who has slotted into the team on an equal footing.

Our evident compatibility is a comfort. Each February advertisements are placed for temporary staff to operate Scott Base and support its annual science programme. Interviews are conducted throughout the country and selection is based on job skills, as well as an ability to form part of a team working in isolation. The team is announced in June and, following a comprehensive medical and dental examination, given final clearance to travel to the ice in October.

Selection of the smaller team that will stay on through the winter requires closer scrutiny with the extra demands of winter's isolation.

The annual training camp, prior to fire training each August, involves virtually everyone who will be working at Scott Base for the forthcoming year. About 200 staff, scientists, other workers and defence force personnel assembled at Tekapo's Balmoral Army Camp in 1994.

This camp provides the opportunity to meet those you'll work with and many topics are covered during this five-day orientation. Hours spent sitting on hard chairs in the lecture room are interspersed with the welcome respite of practical sessions. These include introductory snow-craft and field living skills, radio communications, basic firefighting and first aid.

Our winter-over team is subjected to extra analysis in the form of a Myers-Briggs Type Indicator Test conducted by RNZAF psychologist Kevin McKenna. This test's either/or format assesses and quantifies natural preferences. The results determine an individual's extroversion/introversion, sensing/intuition, thinking/feeling and judging/perceiving. Different combinations of the four preferences lead to 16 possible character profiles.

A high degree of tolerance is indicated if preferences are not too polarised and, as expected, our team fits into the middle ground reasonably well. This suggests the team has been well selected: like any successful society we have a good mix of character types. An even balance of extroverts and introverts is important in the sensory-deprived depths of the Antarctic winter.

Friday arrives. It's our final practical. BA gear and kit are laid out: the action commences. I immediately

Camp-out practical during Tekapo's training camp

discover I have two left-hand leather gloves and, not realising, John Williams finds he has two rights. Why is Dave Berry smiling significantly?

Firstly, NZAP facilities services officer Ron Rogers has to be retrieved from a rearranged BA maze. Mission accomplished. A fire behind the fire tower needs to be extinguished. Mission accomplished. Finally, the *pièce de résistance* – a fire in an old car that has an LPG cylinder in the boot. The team attacks as directed, delivering water from the Wajax pump.

Dave Berry sneaks away to a strategically located fire tender with a much more powerful pump, and waits until the task is complete, then lets fire on our hose operators with water. The force of the fire tender's delivery bowls them off their feet and Dave Mitchell receives a whack in the mouth from his buddy's BA cylinder. A sympathetic team render assistance to a man whose cheesy smile has been modified by two broken front teeth.

During cleanup NZAP director Gill Wratt for-

mally offers me the Scott Base winter manager's position. Perfectly delighted with this team, I accept without hesitation. Gill makes the announcement after presenting us with our Scott Base fire crew badges and certificates. Bruce and Tom are fire chief and deputy and John will be my deputy winter manager.

Bruce promptly offers congratulations, despite his own disappointment. Bruce, the only one of our team who has previously wintered at Scott Base, made no secret of the fact he would have enjoyed being winter manager. I accept Bruce's vote of confidence and I'm equally confident he'll be a most valuable contributor.

We depart for home after lunch and farewells at the Brewers Arms at Ferrymead, and have a month to farewell loved ones. Our team have become quite close, especially during the past five days.

Neill has trained many Scott Base fire crews over the years and likes what he's seen. He's convinced we'll have a good year.

3

INCOMING AND OUTCOMING: THE HANDOVER

Grant (Granto) Avery, the outgoing winter manager, continues our introductory tour of Scott Base. 'And up here we have the laundry,' he announces as we clamber up the stairs behind him. 'Do your own washing and, as the sleeping accommodation is through the wall here,' he points. 'The hours are between 0700 and 2200.' A quick mental calculation converts Scott Base's 24-hour time system into understandable terms. Before long, we'll automatically think this way.

'The domestics have priority use during work hours, save water by selecting the appropriate water level, and ...' reaching down for a drying machine's wire mess screen, 'check there's no lint.' Lint is a fire hazard in very warm dry conditions.

On the way out Granto informs us that the washing powder supplied causes skin irritation. 'If this happens, use less, or buy some Lux Flakes from the shop.'

As a pharmacist, I see this problem at home in Central Otago. Skin dehydrates in the dry environment, making it more susceptible to irritants, so regular use of the moisturiser provided will help.

Our tour continues. With so much to observe it's hard to concentrate on what Granto is saying. The excitement coupled with slight apprehension – we are committed to a year here – are distracting. My mind goes back eight and 10 years to previous summers here, and beyond to my first day at boarding school. This place is very much like a boarding school.

Notes distributed to us by psychologist Kevin McKenna, recommending 'talking openly about parting' and 'planning beyond return in a year's time', have helped smooth the way during the emotionally uncomfortable period of detachment. Our hurdles of detachment vary according to circumstance, with Dave and John also having children to farewell. I'm pleased that Liz and I parted at Queenstown's airport when I observe Dave, wife Sharon and son Al's final days together in Christchurch.

During the 1950s-60s crowds gathered at Harewood Airport to farewell the opening flight to Antarctica each season. But only a local Canterbury TV film crew turns up for us and they interview NZAP operations manager Dave Geddes, who's our Senz-rep (senior New Zealand representative) at Scott Base for the first half of the summer.

The monotone greys of a heavy sky and the tarmac are almost perfect camouflage for the grey, four-jet-engined United States Air Force C-141 Starlifter we're waiting to board. Most of the 100 or so Americans on today's flight are Naval Support Force Antarctica (NSFA) personnel, dressed in dull regulation green. Even our bulky blue-issue clothing looks flat in this morning's subdued light. Only the red jackets of the civilian Antarctic Support Associates (ASA) staff stand out like beacons in the murk.

Eight of our winter-over team fly south today, with Dave Geddes and NZAP facilities manager Peter Brookman making up ten. Jan and Scotty are lucky: they get to take tomorrow's flight in a C-5

Boarding C-141 Starlifter on a grey Christchurch morning

Galaxy – the largest of all the aircraft that fly to the ice. It has almost business-class-like comfort with a proper passenger compartment.

We cram into four lengthwise rows of hammock seats in our C-141. Passenger space is tight early in the season because a large amount of freight needs to be moved south. Full Antarctic survival clothing is a must on all flights, and with a large bulging hand-carry bag each, moving around on board is rather awkward. You're lucky if you get to sit near one of the aircraft's few windows. A load master issues us with a brown paper bag containing lunch and a set of foam earplugs.

We settle in for 5½ hours of sitting, standing, reading, eating and snoozing. Talking is difficult over the noise of the engines. We pass 'PSR' (the point of safe return) so will not 'boomerang' (turn back) today.

Just before 1500 we touch down on McMurdo Sound's smooth seasonal sea ice. Two metres of ice easily supports these large aircraft.

From dull grey to a blast of white – welcome to Antarctica! We all fumble for sunglasses with gloved fingers. Sensory overload sets in as we assimilate the expansive grandeur, -18°C temperature and the squeaking of footsteps on super-dry snow. Taste and smell are the only senses denied.

'Good trip?' Eric, Granto, Mess and Westy smile in welcome. Today's opening flight and our unfamiliar faces ring full time on their year at Scott Base, so they are experiencing mixed emotions of exuberance and sadness.

Adrian Hayter, in his book *The Year of the Quiet Sun*, writes of men requesting to remain at Scott Base after their winter of 1964. He concludes that the isolation creates uncertainty, thus making it easier for people to remain in this less complicated environment.

The base welcoming party and our team exchange greetings in a subdued, slightly stilted way. They're clearly acclimatised, their well-worn jeans, slightly soiled jackets hanging unzipped and Canadian

23

Jim McKenzie and others read while some snooze during the 5½-hour flight to Antarctica

Sorrel boots suggestive of a relatively balmy day. By comparison, we look fresh, fully wrapped up in our clean full survival kits. Their faces are pasty and grey with stubble; we sport healthier complexions.

Granto's team have vacated their rooms and moved into Q Hut. Scott Base has been readied for us, but until the official handover on Friday, in three days, we're the visitors.

At Tekapo we were advised that incoming crews should 'bear small gifts rather than big boots'. The handover period can be difficult.

With Granto's introduction complete, we begin sorting out our rooms. Each 2.5m x 3m room accommodates two, and each winter-over shares with one of the summer staff, who arrives later in the week and gets the top bunk.

The bar opens at 1700 sharp to celebrate the start of the new season. We heed the warning on the bar door, written in Japanese, which advises us not to wear our hats or outdoor boots and clothing into

the bar. If you do, a compulsory shout for all in the bar follows, but this pleasure is usually reserved for our McMurdo visitors, who cannot part with their baseball caps.

Over a beer, any distance between our two teams is soon bridged and it becomes apparent that 'big boots' won't unduly upset Granto's team. But we'll still stick to the 'small gifts'.

Outgoing chef Art Bosman hopes that the settled weather will hold for his replacement Scotty's arrival tomorrow as tonight's dinner will then be his penultimate. Today's flight arrived too late for 'freshies' (fresh fruit and vegetables) tonight; nevertheless Art serves a wholesome dinner.

Art takes pleasure from watching the new arrivals receive static zaps off the metallic bain-marie. In this dry, cold environment, any movement while sitting on a plastic dining-room chair, especially if wearing synthetic clothing, imparts a charge. If you reach for a metal spoon lying on the bain-marie (a

conductor) the zap can be impressive. We have been told we must discharge ourselves before using computers or picking up telephone hand-pieces or damage (to the equipment!) can result.

Ten extra at the dinner table is no big deal at Scott Base, as at least once a week a similar number from McMurdo are invited to dine. However, our status as replacements and our unfamiliar faces and Kiwi accents make us more intrusive.

Once dinner is served, Art and several others head for McMurdo. Only half of the team can go, the other half remaining as fire crew, and, as expected, it is suggested that we take over tonight. (Fire crew handover takes place on Friday after a day or two's orientation.) Many of this team have made good friends at McMurdo during winter and they've only a few days left.

The sun starts dipping behind the southern end of the Royal Society Range at about 2300, casting a beautiful yellow-orange glow onto the icy surroundings. There are about three hours of twilight tonight, but in a few more weeks the sun will remain above the horizon all day and night and such dramatic lighting will cease until late summer.

Tom and I are eager for photographs. Dressing takes time and as it's -24°C with a fresh 10-16 knot wind blowing we wrap up well. Armed with cameras, tripods and a selection of lenses, we don't need to venture far as virtually everywhere we look there's a photo.

'Wow!' 'Neat!' 'Look at that!'

Photographing at colder temperatures is quite challenging. Moist breath freezes on viewfinders, making it hard to see, and stiffened lubricants make it harder to rotate focusing and aperture rings. When it gets really cold you have to use two fully-manual cameras and regularly swap for the one warming inside your jacket.

Battery-powered cameras with auto-focus and wind-on mechanisms soon fail in the cold.

This colourful scene is very intoxicating but, knowing we've plenty of opportunity we head to bed – it's been a long day since the 0430 call for breakfast.

I switch out my light but subdued light still fills my room as I've left the window shutters open. Taking another look outside to reassure myself I'm back in Antarctica, I see Mt Erebus standing aloft, bathed in pink. The distant, almost familiar hum of the base's generator lulls me into a restful sleep.

The C-5 Galaxy lands ahead of a forecast weather deterioration, with Jan, Scotty and a number of summer staff aboard. Art is delighted.

Art's handover is, in Scotty's own words, 'no drama, carry on'. Art tells Scotty he's cooking tomorrow and begins packing up his knives; then our Mt Maunganui chef unpacks his. It helps that Scotty worked here during summer and 'Winfly' (the period from end-of-winter flights until summer) of the 1992-93 year.

Our Balclutha belle, Jan, replaces Ange Bocock as the winter domestic. With summer domestics Ava Nathan and Jacqui Steele she will formulate a programme of daily cleaning. Their biggest task is

A C-141 touches down on McMurdo Sound's sea ice

JAN STRATFORD & ALANA MUIR: BREAKING DOWN BARRIERS

Veteran French polar explorer Dr Paul-Emile Victor told reporters in Hobart in December 1964 that women would not be accepted for Antarctic work.

He said: 'The Russians and the Americans have tried, but it did not work out. Women make excellent scientists and they are physically fit to go to such places. However, at Antarctic bases emotional problems would occur between men and women and this would not exactly help our scientific work. We already have enough worries, and I see no reason why we should help to create new ones.'

The next year in Wellington, Admiral Bakutis, Commander of the US Navy Antarctic Support Forces, told women journalists at a press conference that Antarctica would remain the womenless white continent of peace as far as he was concerned. 'I have no intention of rocking the boat at this early stage,' he said.

There was better news in June 1966. Bob Thomson, then Superintendent of the Antarctic Division of the DSIR, told reporters that the division had received many applications from qualified women for a number of research posts in the Antarctic, as well as from several nurses who sought any kind of job where special qualifications were not necessary. He further stated: 'Last year I said the possibility of having women at Scott Base was for the future. Now I believe we will have them there within five years.'

Bob's prediction was fulfilled and Pam Young was the first. Supporting her husband Euan's field research at Cape Bird during most of the summer of 1969-70, she spent little time at Scott Base itself, a blokes' bastion. Thelma Rodgers, the first to winter over in 1978-79, can be credited with that.

We were born in the same town. Friends for nearly 20 years, we shared a love of adventure and fun and our adventurous spirits have taken us far over the years. Now we were ready to experience Scott Base.

Having flatted together in Aussie, having been chased out of tribal land in northern Pakistan by Kalashnikov rife-wielding militants, having survived

Jan Stratford and Alana Muir

being snowed in near the border with Afghanistan and having endured Turkish men continuously pinching our bums, we felt confident to tackle any challenge Scott Base could throw our way.

We'd poured our share of pints, cooked numerous roasts and fry-ups, scrubbed loos, floors and tables in English pubs. We felt sufficiently qualified to work as Scott Base domestics.

If either of us had been give the chance to handpick one person to share our Antarctic experience – the vastness, the peaceful beauty and the opportunity extended to learn about yourself – we would've picked each other. Unfortunately Scott Base requires only one domestic in the winter-over team. Yet we were privileged when NZAP picked one for 1994-95 and the other for 1995-96.

October 1995 was always going to be memorable and a special occasion as two best friends got to hand over. In helping to break down barriers by being two of 18 women who have filled 471 winter-over positions in Scott Base's first 40 years, we feel very proud.

There to experience Antarctica rather than provoke 'emotional problems ... between men and women', our only problem was that three days of handover in the middle of two years gave little time to catch up.

keeping the vast expanses of vinyl flooring throughout the base washed and polished, so Ange offers a few tips regarding the taming of the commercial floor polishers. It seems a deft touch is required to prevent them hurtling into nearby walls. Ange also introduces Jan to her first-aid duties.

The cold hangar and warmer field store will be Tom's workplace this year. As field support officer, Tom will supply all field parties with field food and equipment, maintain this equipment and carry out a number of field-related tasks. During winter he also takes on stores duties. Bruce (Mess) Janes's handover to Tom is sidetracked into much chat about mountain experiences and shared acquaintances from their work in New Zealand's Southern Alps.

Like Scotty, Bruce from Dunedin is very familiar with his duties as our electrician. Replacing Grant (Westy) West, he meticulously works through the length of the base and discusses the changes since his 1990 winter. Bruce's responsibilities include maintaining the base's fire detection and suppression systems.

Bruce's experience will be invaluable to our two Palmerston North engineers, who have the most diverse range of tasks with which to familiarise themselves with during handover.

John, our engineering services manager (ESM), has already had a sneak preview of his responsibilities. He flew down for a week at Winfly, after fire training. Dave Lucas, John's predecessor, continues to introduce operating procedures for the generators and the RO water plant. Providing power, heat, light and water is a big responsibility, especially during winter when little support is available. John, as ESM, will co-ordinate his engineering team's work.

Dave, with his teeth and smile restored, has one of the busiest and dirtiest jobs as base engineer. If it gets your gloves dirty or smells, then it's probably Dave's job. Fuels, waste disposal (sewage and incineration), dusty ventilation ducting, refrigeration,

heating and engineering manufacturing all feature in Dave's job description. Dave is kept entertained during handover by Dom McCarthy's continuous stream of yarns.

Mechanic Joe makes up the fourth member of the winter-over engineering team inhabiting the lower end of the base. Joe is over-awed by the spaciousness of this workshop compared with his brother's country garage at Drummond in Southland, where he's worked during recent years. The rain and wind don't sweep into this one. Jeremy (JR) Ridgen reminds Joe that sometimes he might get his hands cold with repairs out in the field.

Jim McKenzie, as Telecom technician, has the longest handover period. In addition to introducing Telecom's satellite earth station (SES) link, Jim and Eric Trip have to fly to very high frequency (VHF) radio repeater sites during handover. These repeaters are used in the McMurdo Sound area for field-radio communications during summer. Jim, an engineer with Telecom in Christchurch, has been fortunate a technician couldn't be recruited this year.

Science technician Sean Flanagan familiarises himself with the Hatherton Geosciences Laboratory at the top end of the base. Sean and fellow summer technician Steve Thomas have received a month's training with the science organisations that operate experiments at Scott Base and Arrival Heights (the science laboratory situated higher up on Hut Point Peninsula). Sean exercises his inherent patience as fellow Wellingtonian Granto has to juggle the science handover with ongoing base management.

National Institute of Water and Atmospheric Research (NIWA) ozone scientists Steve (Stevo) Wood, Sylvia Nichol and Karin Kreher, and Carlo Valenti from Italy are present to instruct Sean in the use of their instruments. Belinda (Beej) Bennett, the base support officer (BSO), relates the technical aspects of the science programmes she has monitored during winter.

My position differs from those of the rest of the team. My summer will be spent off-base leading the

Winter 1994 comes to an end and Grant Avery lowers his flag

Antarctic Field Training (AFT) programme, then in February I take on the BSO and winter manager duties.

Like Sean, I'm keen to secure some of Granto's precious time, and spend a morning with Beej looking at the varied duties of a BSO. My first priority is to get AFT up and running.

The weather deteriorates as forecast, bringing us our first storm, or 'herbie', with winds gusting at over 50 knots from the south. The blowing snow virtually obliterates any measure of distance and drums against the base's metal cladding. Bad weather can disrupt season opening and handover, but fortunately for us, this system blows out quickly.

At 1630 on Friday 7 October the tattered winter-1994 New Zealand flag is lowered. Granto's team have completed their end-of-season reports and can begin leaving this home to return to another. Scott Base is now ours, but our winter-over team will have to share it for four or five months first.

4

GOING OUTSIDE

Antarctica is a paradox. Its picture-postcard beauty extends a friendliness that draws you out to investigate, but this attractiveness belies the continent's true nature as an extreme harshness man can never tame. Danger lurks constantly. Poor preparation, taking shortcuts or pushing the limits can get you into trouble very easily in this unforgiving arena.

Early October temperatures are still cold so before leaving the comfort of base you need to dress well. New Zealand has always provided very good

TOM HOPKINS

Ian Hawes appreciating his excellent kit of clothing.
Lake Vanda, Winfly 1995

clothing for its programme, which is not surprising considering our reputation for manufacturing some of the best.

Warmth is efficiently achieved by trapping air around the body with layers of garment. The production of lighter synthetic insulating materials such as Polypropylene and Polartech has seen the demise of wool. But one naturally-occurring product, finest duck or goose down, has never been improved upon and when the temperatures really plummet, a down jacket is hard to beat.

Clothing preference is very individual but the basic combination worn over underwear is: a layer of thermal long-sleeved top and long-johns, a second layer of one thick or two thin jackets and trousers or body-length salopettes, then a final windproof layer of jacket and salopettes. The wind causes the most discomfort in Antarctica, so this outer layer is most important. Two sets of windproofs are issued: one set fully insulated and the other wind-shell only.

The footwear supplied includes Sorrels and the bulkier Japanese Mukluks for colder temperatures. Specialised cold-weather mountaineering boots are supplied to field staff.

When people are dressed in Antarctic kit, sunglasses and snow-goggles make them virtually indistinguishable: a favourite hat is usually used to identify the wearer. Balaclavas, neck gaiters, ear warmers and many options of inner or outer gloves are also available. 'Nosewipers', the heaviest-duty outer gloves, have a woolly sheepskin sewn on the back, which is useful for wiping a cold-induced dripping nose.

TOM HOPKINS

The sea ice pressure ridge formations and a population of Weddell seals are the closest off-base attractions.

McMurdo Sound's frozen surface moves with the forces of tide and wind and fractures occur where this ice sheet abuts land, or heavier fixed 'fast ice'. The pressure ridges formed with the collision between the floating ice sheet and land or 'fast ice' are spectacularly photogenic, particularly when the sun hits at a low angle. But pressure ridge areas can also be dangerous, especially when fresh deposits of uncompacted snow hide cracks and holes, much like crevasse danger on glaciers.

Contrary to popular belief, most people selected

REX HENDRY: FLIGHT TE901, 28 NOVEMBER 1979

Anticipation was the theme of the day. We knew the Air New Zealand flight was coming, where it was to fly, what view we could expect later in the day. Cameras were ready, tripods positioned for the best possible postcard picture.

But shortly after midday Gary Lewis, the Vanda base leader, radioed us at Scott Base to let us know that he had spoken with Flight TE901. He called back shortly after, advising that he had lost contact. They had disappeared. McMurdo Station air traffic controllers reported that they had had the plane on HF radio but not VHF, indicating that it was not in 'line of sight' – where it obviously should have been.

We waited. Waited for further contact. We were advised from New Zealand to wait

Rex Hendry

until the point of no return had been reached and then launch a search.

As the only member of the search and rescue team on base at the time I had been briefed for action that evening. The rest of the team – Hugh Logan, Keith Woodford and Darryl Thompson – were, ironically, on a search and rescue exercise 140km away and could not get back in the deteriorating weather.

'The helicopter's about to leave MacTown [McMurdo] soon and will pick you up in about a quarter of an hour.'

My bag was ready: ice-axe, ice-hammer, rope, harness, slings, sleeping bag, snow shovel, down suit, spare clothes, snacks.

It was a bleak, grey night. The sun was obscured by dense cloud.

The helicopter came in, I hopped on board and we headed north, fast. Up front was the US pilot, a veteran of helo operations in Vietnam, and the co-pilot, McLeod from the RNZAF. In the back were three medics from McMurdo, Jose the crewman and me.

Time seemed suspended in frozen animation, even

to work in Antarctica have no alpine experience and during the summer of 1986-87 two Americans, John Smith and Matthew Kaz, were killed when they fell into a crevasse less than 5km from the security of McMurdo.

Bad weather can halt all movement in the field an such conditions can last for days. Winds of over 28 knots can drift loose snow and reduce visibility towards zero. Uniformly overcast conditions over snow-covered surfaces result in 'whiteouts', where no surface or horizon can be defined.

An Air New Zealand DC10 experienced this phenomenon when it crashed into Mt Erebus (*above*) in November 1979, killing 257 people.

though we were moving fast. A plane down, 257 people on board. Something had been sighted on the northern slopes of Mt Erebus. The weather was closing. Horror. Anticipation. Nausea. How are we going to do this?

'There it is,' thundered in my headset.

A smear was visible on the slopes some 5km away. As we closed in on the tail fin the koru blazed like a beacon; a wheel lay nearby. Nothing else was obvious.

We circled low over the destruction. No movement.

'We'll try to go in,' said the pilot. 'To land at the top end. Stand by to get out.'

The helicopter hovered slowly downward, nose pointing uphill, then dipped suddenly. Spun. Whipped sideways. Plummeted. Steadied. Pulled up. Hovered. Lifted. Hovered again.

'Shit, an inversion.' Cold air was streaming down the hill, within 30 feet of the surface. A gale-force wind drove down the slope, invisible from above except for the loss of surface definition.

We circled two, three times.

'Jose, chuck out a flare!'

A red smoke flare hit the snow, billowing obscene colour into the spin-drift.

We tried to come in again. Forty feet, 30, 20. Nose dipped. Tail lurched. We pulled up. The weather was closing fast. Clouds rushed down to meet us. All reference points evaporated into a blank white canvas. We pulled out and headed back to McMurdo.

Next morning Hugh, Keith and Darryl managed to get in as the weather cleared. They confirmed our worst fears: all 257 passengers and crew had died on impact.

Later that day I returned in a small group from Scott Base and we set up a base camp in preparation for the recovery team, already en route from New Zealand.

The rest, as they say, is history.

[Rex Hendry worked in 1979-80 as Scott Base's electrician. He then wintered over as a mountaineer with the British Antarctic Survey at Rothera Base on the Antarctica Peninsula in the early 1980s, returning to Antarctica on the yacht *Northanger* during summer 1986-87. He is presently the Operations Manager, Scott Base.]

Strict safety rules apply to travel away from the immediate vicinity of the base. There are designated routes, usually marked by flags tied onto bamboo poles. Observation Hill and Crater Hill are worthwhile climbing for the views and approved for solo visits, but foot and cross-country ski travel on sea ice routes and the Castle Rock circuit require at least pairs.

Anyone who leaves the base is required to sign out. If you want to venture any further, you must undertake Antarctic Field Training (AFT) first.

The aim of AFT is to make people comfortable and safe while working and living in the field. Training in the 1990s also includes an emphasis on environmental protection. According to your previous experience in Antarctica you may be required to do a full two-day course or a one-day refresher.

The demand for AFT peaks with the main arrival of scientific staff, known as 'event' staff, early in November, and with a second wave arriving immediately after Christmas. On the ice each particular science project is known as an event and is identified with a code, eg Kiwi 131 (K131). AFT often needs to be rescheduled if the weather holds up flights from New Zealand, and course content can be targeted according to need.

Many regular returnees enjoy their day out on AFT. It allows them a day off from thinking about their work and reintroduces or reacclimatises them to working in the field. Some find the day almost a rekindling of a spiritual Antarctic experience, provided the weather is friendly.

This season's AFT instruction team have very complementary skills. Rachel Brown's teaching background has been honed by many years spent at the Outdoor Pursuits Centre near Turangi. Tarn Pilkington's technical mountaineering and search and rescue background have developed while guiding and working with the Mt Cook National Park's mountaineering team. My contribution is previous Antarctic experience. During 1984-85 I worked as a field assistant on a geological expedition in Northern Victoria Land, then in 1986-87 I returned as a field training instructor.

With preparations complete, our first course begins within a week of summer's opening. Tim Haskell's event, coded K131, are keen to get to Inaccessible Island to begin investigating the properties of early-summer sea ice, but first they need a day's refresher training.

With few events arriving during October, this allows most base staff to receive their training, so Bruce, Joe and Sean, along with summer staff Alan Wilson and Mat Mataroa, are scheduled for the first full course. Our introductory evening includes a course lecture, fitting crampons to boots and practising the alpine technique of prussiking.

Field living in Antarctica necessitates not only wearing plenty of clothing but carrying and using a lot of equipment. Next morning it takes well over an hour to pack a mountain of field and safety equipment into or on top of Hagglunds H-26 – a Swedish twin-cabbed, all-terrain, tracked vehicle. Most things take longer here, but practice will certainly speed things up.

With five in the front of H-26 and the rest sharing the back cab with a pile of personal kit bags and other equipment, we establish radio clearance with base and move out.

First up today is sea ice safety. Travelling on sea ice is a new experience for most people. H-26's rubber tracks clatter across the tidal transition area's bumpy wind-glazed ice, then, following the flags, we weave through the system of pressure ridges. The humpy, wind-accumulated snow on the sea ice, along with the drag of softer snow on our vehicle's tracks, restricts our speed to 15-25km/h. The Hagglunds chops up and down through its range of automatic gears.

Cape Armitage is given a wide berth because thinner sea ice sits over a shoal off the point. When travelling on sea ice it's generally better to stay some

Antarctic Field Training: profiling a sea ice crack (top, left); Sean Flanagan after working up a sweat (top, right); snow shelter area with A-frame and Mt Terror in distance (bottom, left); a humble, yet effective, emergency snow mound (bottom, right).

distance out, away from tidal transitions, shoaled areas and headlands with messy crack systems radiating from them.

Sea ice cracks present in two ways. They can be fresh, straight-edged, tension-release cracks, which usually refreeze and present little problem. Or they can be active working cracks that repetitively break and refreeze. Active cracks that spread apart during this process can be dangerous, especially those with a wide arched formation beneath and thinner centres.

Our instruction identifies active cracks and, using a brace and metre-long lengths of bit, we profile cracks for thickness. Policy allows the crossing of active cracks in tracked vehicles only if the ice is thicker than 700mm for at least two-thirds of the track length.

There is a keen wind blowing across Hut Point Peninsula that hurries our work, but for safety's sake,

no short-cuts can be taken. Near Turtle Rock we can cross at the flagged transition onto land, then travel to the Ross Ice Shelf, via Castle Rock.

For the rest of the day we build emergency snow shelters. Igloo-building is a practised art so we aim for simpler but no less effective snow mounds or covered trenches. Snow is a marvellous medium – it can be heaped into a pile then hollowed out to obtain shelter. It is a good insulator and inside an enclosed snow shelter the temperature remains survivable. You have a better chance of survival inside a snow shelter than in a vehicle. Once a vehicle runs out of fuel and its heater stops, its metal body will conduct heat and the temperature will plummet.

Our five students sleep in their shelter overnight but Rachel, Tarn and I have the luxury of the nearby A-frame AFT instructors' hut.

33

Snow and glacier travel: roped together for crevasse travel

This field-living component of the course also looks at tent-pitching in strong winds, cooking in the field and environmental care.

There's one tent permanently pitched at the instruction site with two toilet buckets inside, one for peeing and the other for pooing – a separation process requiring fine control. Back at base, this pee is flushed down the sewerage system and the poo is incinerated. Liquid waste and washing water are dumped into a grey-water barrel.

Day two of the course is colder, with an overnight low of -35.2°C recorded at Scott Base. Our five in their mound have a slow start to the day, whereas Rachel, Tarn and I have enjoyed the warmth of the A-frame's Preway heater!

Joe is unwell with a mystery allergy and fever so he's returned to Scott Base for an examination by McMurdo's medical staff.

The focus for today is snow and glacier travel and crevasse danger. A heavily-crevassed ice-fall area near Scott Base offers the perfect playground. Stepping across seemingly bottomless holes reinforces the value of a climbing rope and safety techniques. The benign-looking slopes above the ice fall are where the two Americans were killed.

The course finishes with an emergency scenario, requiring use of contents of survival bags that are often carried in vehicles or helicopters.

Until the late 1980s AFT, or Survival School as it was known then, was run in conjunction with the American programme, utilising Kiwi mountaincraft instructors and American logistical support. Search and rescue (SAR) continues as a joint operation.

Rachel, Tarn and I, along with our five McMurdo equivalents who run their field training programme, form the Joint Antarctic Search and Rescue Team (JASART) primary team. Secondary and winter teams are drawn from other staff with outdoor experience and they receive training during summer.

SAR requires good teamwork, so the moment our Tekapo training was finished, the three of us and NZAP field operations officer Eric Saxby were whisked away by helicopter to the upper Tasman Glacier in Mt Cook National Park for two days. Tarn familiarised us with the latest crevasse rescue techniques he acquired during his summer at Mt Cook.

Crevasse accidents, aircraft accidents and searching for overdue people are the most likely Antarctic SAR scenarios. Twice a month we join our JASART colleagues from McMurdo for day training sessions, practising working with helicopters, stretcher rescue from crevasses and off steep snow or rock slopes, first aid, and navigation using Global Positioning System (GPS) and Radio Direction Finder (RDF) aids.

One afternoon in November the weather suddenly deteriorates and while I'm enjoying dessert I'm summoned to the phone. Base services manager (BSM) Graham White has field training instructor Brooks Montgomery from McMurdo on the line. A SAR has been called.

'This is a heads up, this isn't an exercise,' are his first words. 'We have a missing person on the sea ice on a snow-mobile, no radio, no survival bag. We're pulling the gear from our locker,' completes his brief message. A procedure is in place for us to follow.

Communications operator Gloria Mooney almost simultaneously receives the official call from Mac Ops (McMurdo Operations, used as our SAR operations centre) and activates our SAR pagers. Their piercing beeps are chilling.

Matters are complicated by key people being off base. Senzrep Dave, who would normally co-ordinate our JASART involvement from Mac Ops, is in

New Zealand and his standby, operations support manager (OSM) Alan Wilson, is caught out in the Miers Valleys because of the weather. JASART member Rachel is presently sitting in Hagglunds H-28 out on the sea ice with Eric, John and plant operator Addy Atkins. They, on their way to Tim Haskell's sea ice field camp, can't move either because of the weather.

Tom joins our team and he and Tarn take Hagglunds H-26 to the Berg Field Centre to pack equipment. Graham stands in as SAR co-ordinator and he and I drive to Mac Ops for planning and briefing.

Launching from the BFC, Tom joins Americans Steve, Bill, Buck and medic Fritz in the Americans' Hagglunds 002, while Tarn and I join Brooks, Mike (a Kiwi working for the Americans) and medic Turk in H-26. With enough rescue, survival and medical

JASART activity: working with a UH-1N Huey on Observation Hill (top); Charlie Brumbaugh, and David Khoo below, attend to my stretcher during a crevasse rescue exercise (below).

PAUL P....... RESCUE : THE TRUE STORY

WE JOIN THE STORY AS OUR FEARLESS JASART HEROES ARE STUMBLING BUMBLING NAVIGATING BLINDLY PRECISELY AROUND THE ROSS SEA ICE SEARCHING FOR LOST AMERICAN BEAKER PAUL P...... THE RAGING GROUND BLIZZARD RAGES.......

RACHEL BROWN and TARN PILKINGTON

equipment, and food and fuel for almost a week, we depart within two hours of notification. Thorough preparation takes time.

Paul, the missing scientist, checked out from McMurdo at 1400 with the intention of travelling 35km to his field camp, the Solar Barn. His estimated time of arrival was 1600. He failed to show up and the first SAR for 1994-95 has been called.

We sweep the closely flagged route heading towards Cape Evans, with a vehicle driving either side and managing to keep visual contact with the flags. The side windows quickly ice up, obscuring any view, so we take turns standing aloft through each vehicle's roof hatch in an effort to scan for the snowmobile and Paul.

From the turnoff to the Solar Barn at Junction 14 the flags are further spaced – about 200-300m. Conditions verge on whiteout, but lulls between the 20-30 knot gusts extend visibility to 50-100m, which allows us to locate the flags. Without GPS and Buck Tily's knowledge of the sea ice conditions in this area we wouldn't be out here. We fix many GPS waypoints. While Brooks had been observing he spotted a lone Adelie penguin on the downwind side, not too far back.

Just before midnight the Solar Barn appears from out of the murk and Paul hasn't been located. His colleagues offer hot drinks while we contemplate our next move. If only he had a radio, we could be using our RDF.

'I've got a hunch,' suggests Brooks. Apart from a systematic grid search there aren't too many alternatives. He suggests a random-scattter search downwind near the penguin. We have GPS way-points to take us back to the flagged route and Buck's comforting assurance that the ice here in the centre of McMurdo Sound is pretty good. This is looking for a needle in a haystack kind of stuff.

Bill McCormack atop Hagglunds 002 during a whiteout search for Paul (top); finding the US Solar Barn camp during the search (below).

We have to accept the risk of blindly driving in a whiteout as there is a life at stake. It's comforting to know that Hagglunds do float, if only for a short while.

Luck is on our side. At 0126, about half an hour after we leave the Solar Barn, both Hagglunds zero in on the desolate speck of a snow-mobile, with Paul huddled under its cover. Mildly hypothermic and hungry, he's lucky temperatures have remained above the -15°C recorded during this period. The storm lasts a further two days.

Towards the end of summer a fellow American isn't so fortunate. Our JASART team recovers his body after a fall off Castle Rock.

5

IN SUPPORT OF SCIENCE

When we were on the ice, NZAP, a division of the Ministry of Foreign Affairs and Trade, had the responsibility for supporting New Zealand's science in Antarctica. This responsibility has since been taken over by the government agency Antarctica New Zealand. In 1994-95 NZAP was allocated $5.11 million to fund operations both in New Zealand and Antarctica. Flight support, the most expensive facet of the programme this year, cost just over $1 million. Twenty-six science events were supported with this money.

New Zealand is greatly advantaged by having the United States Antarctic Programme (USAP) launching its major operation out of Christchurch. We can piggyback on its regular air link with Antarctica – a luxury most other national programmes don't have. The alternatives are five hours in a C-141 or up to two weeks on a ship. The arrangement with USAP means many scientists supported by our programmes can make quick forays to the ice.

There has to be a good reason to conduct science in Antarctica and generally approval is forthcoming only if similar work cannot be conducted elsewhere. Environmental issues loom large. Will the impact on the environment outweigh any realistic result? Will the event budget provide for environmental considerations, such as transporting wastes from the field?

The Ross Dependency Research Committee, a government advisory board, used to consider all proposals and decide which events would be supported. That job now falls to Antarctica New Zealand. These days financial constraints are limiting the scale and length of most operations, which ironically helps limit the impact on the environment.

Most scientists happily tolerate reduced comforts, living in tents and cooking their own food while in the field. They would prefer their precious funds to go towards extra helicopter hours or better science facilities back at base.

But this hasn't always been the case. Captain James Cook made a concerted effort to solve the puzzle of Terra Australis Incognita, the speculated land mass at the bottom of the world. He set sail in 1772 minus Joseph Banks, the eminent scientist and socialite. Cook and the Admiralty both wanted Banks on the voyage, and Banks wanted to go, but only under certain conditions. Banks objected to the accommodation on Cook's boat *Resolution*. Cook even offered him his own quarters, but there wasn't enough room for Banks's entourage of 13, including two french horn players to entertain the scientist in the manner to which he was accustomed.

The Admiralty built a boat big enough to accommodate Banks's wishes but it was so top heavy it was deemed unseaworthy. Banks was left at home.

To my knowledge no french horn players have yet accompanied New Zealand scientists on their Antarctic missions!

The international science fraternity's efforts in the International Geophysical Year 1957-58 will be remembered not only for their scientific success but also for their contribution to world harmony. IGY helped diffuse mounting international tension amid Cold War-related moves to secure or consolidate Antarctic territorial claims during the 1950s.

DR TREVOR HATHERTON OBE, DSC, DIC, FRSNZ. 1924–92

'As leader of the IGY contingent, Hatherton had the overall responsibilities of his team, and in addition undertook to cover two aspects of investigation himself. During the longer winter period he took the auroral observations. Although for this purpose he had erected an all-sky camera, which consisted of a camera so mounted as to be able to photograph the whole sky, he found that there was no better way of recording the changes in an auroral display than by getting out through an astro-hatch with a notebook and pencil – a chilling experience with temperatures far below zero.'

– *Antarctica*, A.S. Helm and J.H. Miller

At the time noted above, this Yorkshire-born geophysicist, a dedicated and modest man, was beginning a life-long involvement in Antarctic science. It is recorded that Dr Trevor Hatherton discovered, for all of the cloudless days from mid-May to mid-August during the winter of 1957, that aurorae occurred on all bar two. Some lasted for up to six hours and the highest probability occurred between the cheerless hours of 0400 and 0500. He must have spent many hours out through the astro-hatch.

Trevor arrived in New Zealand in 1950, was awarded his PhD in 1953 and joined the Geophysics Division of the DSIR.

His desire to work in Antarctica was fulfilled in the summer of 1955-56 when he travelled south with the Americans' first Operation Deep Freeze. His task, with geologist Bernard Gunn and navy photographer Bill Smith, was to find a site for Scott Base and reconnoitre a route up on to the Polar Plateau for the Trans-Atlantic Expedition.

The site they selected for Scott Base was at Butter Point. Trevor returned the following summer as leader for International Geophysics Year (IGY), wintering over in 1957. As the *HMNZS Endeavour* couldn't get in near Butter Point, Scott Base was built near McMurdo Station at Pram Point.

Trevor Hatherton

On his return, Trevor became a member of the newly-established RDRC and in 1958 he visited the United States to discuss scientific and logistical collaboration between the US and New Zealand. This was the start of his 30-year involvement with the RDRC, culminating with his being chairman from 1983 to 1989.

Trevor was the director of the Geophysics Division of the DSIR from 1967 to 1985, when he relinquished the position to concentrate on research until his retirement in 1989.

He became president of the Royal Society of New Zealand (1985-89) and was the driving force behind the establishment in 1987 of the Antarctic Heritage Trust, of which he became patron.

Despite his tongue-in-cheek comments about women in Antarctica, he was very supportive in getting women scientists to the ice.

Trevor Hatherton was awarded the Queen's Polar medal and an OBE in 1958, and will be permanently remembered by the Antarctic community through the Hatherton Geosciences Laboratory at Scott Base, which he opened soon after his retirement.

In the summer of 1992-93 Trevor's ashes were spread from a helicopter over the Ferrar-Taylor glacier confluence, to which he had walked 37 years earlier.

The spirit of IGY's sharing of both data and logistical support was the precursor to the development of the Antarctic Treaty, which took effect in 1961. This treaty has contributed as a safeguard against international tension and also provided a forum for implementation of laws to provide environmental protection, the Madrid Protocol being the latest addition.

Much of IGY's research, which focused on upper atmospheric and earth physics, has continued since 1957. Ongoing seismological, geomagnetic, ionospheric and meteorological observations have run continuously at Scott Base.

In other areas of research there has been a change of focus. In the 1950s-60s the main interest was in exploratory geological and mapping projects. Parties made long dog-sledge trips to far-reaching areas of the Ross Dependency, with one dog team covering 2500km in one season! These trips required much logistical support and parties were required to be in the field for most of the summer.

An emphasis of science today is towards environmental impact, for example ozone hole formation and global warming. Today data logger and satellite technology mean less time in the field. Technicians can monitor experiments on behalf of the scientists back in New Zealand.

During summer Scott Base becomes a melting-pot of scientific interests. Words such as antifreeze protein, spectrometer, thermophilic and glacio-tectonic are dropped into breakfast-table conversation. Scientists come from New Zealand universities, government and private research organisations, often with collaborators from other countries.

As well as science, support is given to publicity, works projects and historic site preservation events.

Independent Television News (ITN) of Great Britain has been invited to Antarctica by NZAP to give New Zealand's science programme some international exposure. Reporter Jo Andrew and cameraman Peter Wilkinson arrive during November 1994 to film a series of four ITN News at Ten items reporting on science, the environment and historical conservation.

NZAP information manager Tim Higham and I support their trips into the field.

We make maximum use of the 180 hours of RNZAF time contributed to the United States/New Zealand programme's helicopter logistic pool. The RNZAF Iroquois 'Squadron 03' crew – Rangi Pirihi, Keith Buckley and Darren Goodwin – load a complete field camp aboard their machine: food, kitchen and primus boxes, first-aid kit, sleeping kits, field mattresses, personal kit bags, field radio, small dome tent, field safety equipment, small fuel-spill kit and two toilet buckets. A polar tent is too big to go inside so is fastened to a skid.

Dissotichus mawsoni in a McMurdo science fish tank

A Weddell seal visits John Macdonald's fish-hut hole

Peter Wilkinson filming for ITN, on the Dais in the Dry Valleys

With radio clearance from Scott Base, Rangi applies the power and we lift off. A piercing hooter alerts everyone that a helicopter is operating on the helo pad. The rotor wash sprays small scoria particles everywhere and Tom, still close at hand after helping us load the machine, receives a mild sandblasting.

In broken cloud we fly on GPS towards the Dry Valleys. The frozen surface of McMurdo Sound below is lined with random crack systems and most surface texture is obliterated because of the cloud. Rounding the Kukri Hills on the mainland, we enter the Taylor Dry Valley.

The Dry Valleys are unique. Strong katabatic winds flowing off the 3000m Polar Plateau to the west warm up as they descend to sea level. Snow in the valleys, deposited by moister coastal easterlies, evaporates. This ice-free area is regarded as being one of the driest places on earth.

Peter pans the beauty with camera and comments that the lowering clouds are adding mood. We fly across the Asgaard Range to New Zealand's Vanda Station (established in 1968) beside Lake Vanda in the Wright Valley.

The Asgaard Range features in New Zealand's Antarctic folklore. Kiwis hydrologists, or the Asgaard Rangers as they became known, made annual surveys of the glaciers on this range through the 1970s-80s. During summer, melt from these glaciers forms rivers, which flow into lakes such as Lake Vanda.

It seems the Asgaard Rangers, with Viking-like demeanour, had a habit of descending to pillage food from the 'Vandals' (Vanda Station's inhabitants). Vandals were, apparently, higher life-forms as the station was supplied with fresh food rather than dried field food. (Of course the Asgaards dispute the higher life-form bit, arguing that it was because they worked at a higher altitude.)

Before we descend to Vanda we land on the Dais, a superb viewpoint looking east down the Wright Valley and west up to the Polar Plateau.

Two events are present at Vanda Station. Clive Howard-Williams and Mark James of NIWA (K081)

Lake Vanda and the old Vanda Station (left); Operation Safari demolishes Vanda laboratory (right).
Opposite: Lake Vanda in Wright Valley, with its extremely photogenic four-metre thick ice.

are working on the lake's ecology, and Operation White Safari are decommissioning the station. A team from the Royal New Zealand Navy, under the direction of carpenter Cullum (Scully) Boleyn, are here for a month. Scully will return to complete the task after New Year, with a group from the New Zealand Army. Lake Vanda has risen 10m in a decade. With the prospect of flooding, decreased science in this valley and unnecessary environmental impact, Vanda Station is going.

Jo and Peter have two days to cover such issues as possible global warming causing the lake's rising, the environmental reconditioning of the station site, and any other human impact on these valleys.

Clive and Mark are sampling at the other end of the lake, having drilled through 4m of hard fresh-water lake ice. Lake Vanda is about 70m deep at their site. The sun's radiation is absorbed through the clear ice and water and this energy becomes trapped in the undisturbed layers of increasing salinity below. The temperatures at the base of the lake are close to +25°C! They are investigating what impact the added meltwater (the extra 10m) is having on algae growing in the layer of salinity known as the Deep Chlorophyll Maximum (DCM) (60-65m).

Clive claims Lake Vanda's year-round seal of lake ice offers the unique opportunity to conduct research in water where there is no mixing due to wind.

After two days an American UH-1N Huey helicopter picks us up. We spend 20 minutes on the ground at Bull Pass, the site of some brilliant wind-eroded and contorted ventifact rocks. Cloud produces

Lake Vanda ice

ET? A two-metre tall ventifact rock at Bull Pass

soft lighting and some light snow precipitation adds
to the mood.

Any film clip of Antarctica needs penguins, so we
fly a considerable distance north to locate some
emperors at the ice edge of McMurdo Sound. Sea
ice conditions are particularly heavy this year. The
excitement mounts as we approach the white/blue
boundary of ice edge. The dots of birds in ones or
twos give a measure of scale and our height above
the sea ice. A group is located.

Before shutting down the helicopter on the sea
ice, some distance from both the birds and the ice
edge, the crewman probes at length at the ice with
his ice axe. It's safe. So is the ice all they way to the
edge.

Emperors spend summer feeding at the ice edge
before migrating to land-based breeding colonies
during winter. The males need to store plenty of
body fat as they face four miserable months with-

A penguin-shaped pressure ridge

out food while they incubate their partners' eggs.
Such fasting can result in almost a halving of body
mass. The large emperors have had to adapt to breed
through winter because the incubation and rearing
of large chicks can not fit into the summer season.

Antarctic wildlife protection protocols preclude
us from approaching within 5m of the penguins but
they are not bound by rules. While we're sitting on
the ice their curiosity gets the better of them and
they waddle to almost within touching distance. It's
obvious they have little to fear out of the water.

We spend two entertaining hours photographing these clowns of the Antarctic. One of my objec-
tives this season has been satisfied – on my first two
visits I didn't see any emperors.

Early in December research meteorologists Tom
Clarkson and Tom Kerr (K088) require a balloon
launcher. I have no AFT scheduled for a few days so
I oblige and am treated to some entertainment on
line-of-sight Channel Six VHF.

The Toms, from NIWA, are investigating the
deposition of airborne pollutants from Scott Base's
generator and incinerator exhaust. Low-level prevailing air currents over Scott Base are determined
by flying delicately-weighted tetroon (four-sided)
balloons in light winds. The data gathered will determine future snow sampling sites.

Each Tom, using a tracking theodolite, is positioned at a particular fixed point on the Ross Ice

An emperor penguin – the clown of Antarctica

Meteorologist Tom One about to launch a tetroon while a distant Tom Two waits with his tracking theodolite

Shelf and they use VHF radios to communicate. They are both calmly spoken and stoic, and in dry humour they identify themselves as Tom One and Tom Two. The ensuing chit-chat is almost 'nerdish' as they're gripped intensely by their scientific endeavour:

'Tom Two, Tom Two, this is Tom One, how copy? Over,' precisely worded.

'Roger Tom One, this is Tom Two, reading you loud and clear, over,' equally precise.

'Roger Tom Two, did ya get that one?' relaxing a little.

'Yeah, Tom One, that's a good one,' excitement barely suppressed.

'Yeah, that one went over Crater Hill,' open excitement. As if we didn't notice.

'Roger Tom,' momentarily forgetting the numeral, 'the wind has obviously changed.' The previous five flights have all headed towards Cape Armitage.

'Do you think we need another, Tom Two?'

'No, Tom One, we have enough, and wind is changing, over.'

'Yeah, Tom Two, we've enough, I'll just call Warren … Warren, Warren, this is Tom One, how copy? Over.'

Suppressing the urge to laugh, I quickly acknowledge, climb onto my snow-mobile and scoot across the undulating snows towards them.

By mid-January most event staff are here and the need for AFT has come almost to an end. Rachel and I share the provision of field support for Waikato University's Hugh Morgan and his two German collaborators, Juergen Wiegel and Karl O. Stetter (K025). These specialist microbiologists are here to sample volcanically-heated ground for thermophilic bacteria.

Volcanically-warmed snow-free areas near the summits of Mt Erebus and Mt Melbourne (400km to the north near Terra Nova Bay) are so isolated that they can be sampled and compared with other

45

Microbiologists Juergen Wiegel and Karl O. Stetter sampling volcanic soil on Mt Melbourne's Crytogram Ridge

more accessible sites on earth. More exciting is the prospect of isolating a new species.

Rachel supports the team near the summit of Erebus; inclement weather dogs them for the week.

Another Waikato University team, Dieter Adam and Tracy Dale, with Pat Selkirk from Australia's Macquarie University (K022), are determining genetic variations in Antarctic mosses. Their event takes them to nine geographic locations in the Ross Sea area, including Mt Melbourne and Edmonson Point, also near Terra Nova Bay.

Our transport, RNZAF Kiwi Iroquois '03', is held up for a day while a new engine is refitted. The final flight crew of the season, Paul Stockley, Stu Brownlie and Ty Cochran, fly us north. With K022 and K025 both on the one flight, limited space means Hugh and Tracy have to stay behind.

One of our field camps has already been dispatched to the Italian Base at Terra Nova Bay. Earlier in the month Antarctic Heritage Trust staff Neville Ritchie and Roger Fyfe visited the Inexpressible Island, just to the south of Terra Nova Bay, to examine a depot originally left by Scott's Northern Party. They took our field camp.

It's a squeeze in the helicopter with one extra. Helicopter mechanic Grant Bennie has to accompany us to give the new engine its five-hour check before returning from Terra Nova Bay. Our 2½-hour flight to Terra Nova Bay requires two refuellings, at Marble Point and Depot Island.

We cover 400km of broken sea ice and heavily-crevassed ice-tongue glaciers flowing off the coast. What a long way to walk, especially if you have just spent winter living in an ice cave eating meagre rations supplemented with seal meat. Scott's Northern Party did just that, having spent the winter of 1912 at Inexpressible Island after sea ice conditions prevented their ship returning to pick them up. Their

Our camp on Mt Melbourne near midnight

arduous trip back to Scott's hut at Cape Evans took 40 days – the effort made bitter-sweet by the news that Scott and his men had perished on their return from the Pole, before winter.

Flying this distance with the security of regular radio communication with base gives us a real appreciation of technological advance. We continue on to the modern Italian base.

From Terra Nova Bay Station Dieter and Pat are flown to Edmonson Point, then Juergen, Karl and I are flown to the top of Mt Melbourne's (2700m) dormant cone. Terra Nova Bay's sea-level temperatures of close to zero reduce by about 10°C on the mountain.

The summit area on top of Mt Melbourne is gazetted as a Site of Special Scientific Interest (SSSI). Special guidelines restrict operations in these areas, and at this site attempts are made to reduce the introduction of foreign micro-organisms by disinfect-

ing boots and implements used on snow-free areas, and by wearing aseptic protective oversuits.

I pitch two tents overlooking the volcano's glacier-filled caldera and begin melting snow for water and hot drinks. Juergen and Karl venture onto Cryptogram Ridge to begin sampling. Their probe registers at +64°C half a metre below the surface, a temperature close to optimum for thermophilic bacterial growth. The chaps are happy.

Mt Melbourne provides stunning views. Open sea to the east is a real treat after months of looking at frozen oceans in McMurdo Sound. To the north Mt Murchison dominates, then the landward sweep south is just miles and miles of peaks and ranges. A long Campbell Glacier Ice Tongue protrudes and floats on open water, and Terra Nova Bay is further south beyond it.

Juergen and Karl sample until late and dinner is eaten close to midnight.

Juergen and Karl, replete and satisfied with their day's work, are ready for bed

Iroquois '03' arrives the following morning with Dieter and Pat for their 24 hours on the mountain. Juergen and Karl return to Scott Base happy with their samples, and Karl, who claims he's isolated the organism that produces perfect sauerkraut, only can wonder what he may have found on Mt Melbourne.

Dieter and Pat take samples from Cryptogram Ridge's warmed soils, where a reasonably prolific population of *Campylopus* moss grows. It's amazing that vegetation can grown at such an altitude in such low air temperatures – our minimum thermometer drops to -25°C while we're on the mountain. Small steaming fumarole ice chimneys add a feeling of warmth but, gazing into their dark depths, one isn't keen to venture any closer.

The weather holds into the third day and high-frequency (HF) radio communication with Scott Base advises that '03' should be with us in an hour.

We strike camp, take a few more photos of a place very seldom visited, and wait.

'03' lands at Terra Nova Bay just before midday – perfect timing for an invitation to lunch. Midday Sunday signals half a day's rest for the Italians, who work very long hours, and the occasion is celebrated with a decent lunch and a few bottles of chianti (cask wine is the usual). The selection of pastas, king prawns, fresh salad then espresso with sweet chocolate is a far cry from the 1912 Inexpressible Island ice cave meal of seal meat and more seal meat.

We sit with three New Zealand helicopter pilots – Ben Gower, John Dickson and Phil Todhunter – who work for Helicopters New Zealand, the Nelson company that has the contract to fly for the Italians. We're asked to send more Steinlager if any flights are coming up this way. These lads are not so keen on chianti.

6

A Day in the Life of Scott Base

November 8, 1994. The past week's frustrations – a 72-hour 'herbie', five days with no incoming flights, and accumulating hoards of impatient event staff in Christchurch – are now easing. Things are finally happening.

Lynette Simmonds, the senior communications (comms) operator, has been on watch since midnight. No one has called. Daylight has streamed in the radio room's windows all night – two weeks have elapsed since the sun's last setting; yet early morning sun still casts a lovely texture on the white expanses.

Lynette's attentions have been elsewhere – there's been another replay of *Four Weddings and a Funeral* on the video. A couple of dirty coffee cups point to a long night.

'Morning, Lynette.'

OSM Alan has successfully tiptoed the gauntlet of squeaking flooring down the hallway of the accommodation block. Low humidity dries the timber and makes it squeak. Down in the command centre Alan dons his jacket, grabs his folder and kit bag of emergency clothing and takes the keys for Toyota T-31. He signs out in the book at 0645, to return at 0745. Destination? 'Helo Ops' (helicopter operations) meeting at 0700 at Mac Ops.

This is Alan's first meeting for a week. He has enjoyed a sojourn in the Miers Valley on the mainland with carpenters Dan Keller and Gary (Gazza) Smith, and cargo handler Mat. Their overnight mission to dismantle the Miers hut lasted a week. Their weather was good, but not so ours on Ross Island – no helicopter could fly to collect them. Alan, who empathises with the outdoors, could have stayed longer, but not Mat.

Scott Base requires only one helicopter movement this afternoon – Otago University geologist Yvonne Cook and field assistant Danny Higgins (K061) are flying into the Ferrar Glacier area. Alan has to plan for the onslaught later in the week, particularly the mountain of equipment Allan Green's group (K024) needs flown to Granite Harbour.

Three or four walking the squeaking flooring each morning wake the rest. Through the double fire doors and down some stairs is the ablutions block – women to the left and men to the right. Courteous morning greetings are exchanged. Water runs and splashes in handbasins and showers. Toilets flush. There's farting, yawning and tuneless whistling. Such is the activity of a communal bathroom – the world is waking up!

One or two new faces are noticed – territorial feelings are developing after only a month.

Event staff get an earlier morning call with Q Hut's even squeakier floors but that's no problem as they are highly motivated to maximise their limited time at Scott Base.

Breakfast starts at 0700 but most traipse in later, timing their arrival to allow just enough time to eat before they head to work at 0758.

The perverse music of Yello on the stereo in the mess is first turned down then off – Scotty's taste in music falls well short of his food.

First, a cold drink. The drinks machine offers a choice of chilled water or two flavours of cordial. A look out the windows reveals a beautiful clear day.

The New Zealand flag on the flagpole flutters gently, confirming the five knots of prevailing north-easter registering on the anemometer dials in the mess. Of greater interest, a digital thermometer reads -15.2°C. We're in for a balmy day. Temperatures start climbing in November.

A selection of cereals and fruits predominates the servery at breakfast and this morning some fresh fruit salad is offered. In the bain-marie a lone pot of porridge is kept warm. Diets have changed over the years. There are no bacon and eggs dripping in fat or baked beans or spaghetti on offer, but Scotty takes a few orders for cooked breakfast.

A selection of commercially-baked grain breads keep the six-slice toaster busy – the timer runs continuously as more slices are added. Regular flights during summer ensure a good supply of bread and fresh food.

Ang Tutua takes on the 0800-1600 comms shift, which allows Lynette to get something to eat before bed.

Two who are in no great hurry this morning are carpenter Dan Keller and scientist Sylvia Nichol (K085). Their bags are packed for an 0930 'bag drag' (baggage check-in) for this afternoon's turnaround flight back to Christchurch. Despite the weather being fine at this end yesterday, the flight was rescheduled until today because of mechanical malfunction. Dan and Sylvia have been here since Winfly in August. They'll be missed.

Dan is the first of our support staff 'family' to leave this season, and he departs bestowed with not only the nickname Blossom, but also the title of 'legend', after satisfying certain criteria laid down this season. During training in August he had predicted that he was going to 'positively blossom' with this experience – the nickname has stuck and the experience delivered.

Waiting-in-the-wings 'legend' number two, summer mechanic Dennis Ham, walks down to the lower end of the base with some of his engineering team-

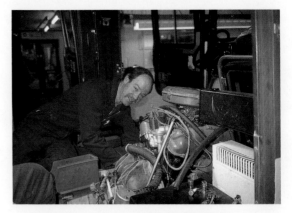

Summer mechanic and legend Dennis Ham

mates. John clarifies what each has planned for the day, then heads into the foyer outside the powerhouse. Selecting the best set of earmuffs, he makes a quick inspection of his 'babes' (generators) and the RO water plant. After a month he's becoming tuned to the machinery's idiosyncrasies.

Graham sorts through the vehicle allocation for the day. He holds all the keys in his BSM's office and, during busier times, takes bookings for vehicles. Science takes priority over recreation and this applies to vehicle use too.

Now in November, the Americans have commenced their regular shuttle bus service to Scott Base for shoppers. Once the Williams Field ice shelf runway opens later this month, when the sea ice is considered too soft to land aircraft on, hourly shuttles servicing the field will pass our bus shelter 24 hours a day. We can use these shuttles too.

At 0815, Senzrep Dave meets with Alan, Graham and John in his office for the day's management meeting. Today there's much to catch up on and recent hold-ups will see some rescheduling. Graham has just received an e-mail from Christchurch, from NZAP movements controller Woody, advising that 11 'pax' (personnel) are heading south today and have an ETA of 1430. Sleeping quarters have been allocated and the chefs will be advised.

Alan presents his proposed rescheduled operations forecast for the week. John is happy.

Pressure ridges in front of Scott Base form dramatic shapes in differing lights

Top: A golden Blue Glacier taken from Observation Hill. Bottom: The sea refreezing in March. The Royal Society Range is in the background.

Steve needs little more than a coat and light gloves when outside reading the Stevenson met screen at 0900. The thermometers read: current -13.5°C, maximum (yesterday) -8.9°C and minimum (early this morning) -18.5°C. At the top of the met tower Steve checks the pyranometers recording global, direct and diffuse radiation. He also spies engineer Dave making his morning inspection.

Dave checks his fuel tanks, water tanks, and both the sewage outflow and seawater intake daily. Heat traces around these pipes keep them flowing. Later in the day American Larry Brown will slowly drive across with a couple of loads of JP-8 in his Fuel Mule. Dave and Larry are getting on well, and with Larry wintering too, the smile on Dave's face is of approval.

0915. Graham is too busy to drive Dan and Sylvia to McMurdo for bag drag so postal/admin clerk Jo Kilpatrick takes them, as well as a good-sized bag of outward mail. A new release of Ross Island stamps last week has kept us busy with philatelic requests and a special Scott Base postmarking of these stamps.

Before 1000 the first shuttle bus from McMurdo drops off a few shoppers, and while waiting in the visitors' area outside the shop they help themselves to a coffee from the Cafe Bar.

The Armed Forces Canteen Council (AFCC) from New Zealand runs the shop and bar facility at Scott Base and manager Shaun Smith is back for his third summer.

Shaun, affectionately known as Mattress Back, opens the shop late again, but soon makes up lost time with masterly craftsmanship. A shopper after the latest stamps might leave with a new T-shirt, compact disc or maybe even a souvenir teaspoon. New stock trickles in on most flights, space permitting.

At 1000 it's smoko time in the engineers' smoko room, a place where dirty overalls and boots are permitted. It's fairly congested at this time of year and Scotty's morning tea is not ready at 1000 sharp this morning. When Ava arrives with a big tray of scones topped with jam and cream she retorts, 'It's not my bloody fault.' Not surprisingly, Scotty has been busy on the phone again. She leaves the gannets to it, including Dan, who is back in time for his last morning smoko with the boys.

There are scones left over in the mess where the rest have their morning tea.

Jan, Ava and Jacqui have quickly established a workable domestic routine and Senzrep Dave has already told them they rate among the best. This week Jacqui's assisting in the kitchen and mess, Jan's cleaning the upper base, including the ablution area, and Ava has the lower end.

It's a beautiful day out at the AFT snow shelter area. This course is the biggest so far, with 13 (or 14 if you count Thingee of Television New Zealand fame). The TVNZ crew are filming presenters Aaron Devitt and Thingee for children's programmes *What Now?* and *Son of a Gunn*.

Taking H-26, Rachel and Tarn continue with today's AFT with, first, a Dry Valley module up at Castle Rock, then later a sea ice module. Our course the format has been modified since last month.

With Yvonne and Danny (K061), all the sleeping kits used last night and the toilet buckets and grey-water barrel I return to Scott Base in H-16.

Jan with a polisher firmly under control

Yvonne and Danny have to assemble their field kit for a 1530 flight this afternoon.

Approaching Scott Base I give way to our two army 'planties' (plant operators), Shane (Addy) Atkins and Lindsay (Tails) Taylor who are operating the D5 and D8 bulldozers. They continue to remove many cubic metres of snow accumulated behind the base during the winter. The herbie last week has provided a small top-up. Addy, plugged into some Kamahl on his Walkman and smiling enthusiastically, gives a big 'hang loose' wave as he passes on the D5.

I have a few things to sort out for a meeting with Dave this afternoon, but first I hang the sleeping kits in the field drying room to air. Each kit, an inner inserted inside another bag, plus a bag cover, has to be separated and hung up. Static shocks are guaranteed.

Tom's unheated hangar is now warming considerably, making life much more comfortable for him. Not that he has time to think about the cold at the moment, as many field events will be supplied in the next week or two. Yvonne and Danny are impressed to find that he as most of their equipment piled on a small trailer, ready to go.

Tom is attending to botanist Allan Green. Allan's high-tech event has an elaborate array of electronic scientific equipment, so since they're taking a generator, they have a coffee machine and microwave packed too. We've come a long way since Scott's expedition of 1912!

Allan has also made provision for his student, Kadmiel Maseyk, to sit one of his University of Waikato examination papers while at Granite Harbour. No doubt this paper will be remembered for many years to come.

Lunchtime aromas percolate from the mess. Summer chef Scott Taylor has surfaced and has had to take over the lunch preparation from his winter equivalent Scotty because NZAP purchasing officer Helen Boerlage, in Christchurch, has phoned earlier and requested Scotty's 'freshies' order before lunch. The kitchen will be required to impress the distinguished visitors (DVs) arriving later this week – members of Parliament John Carter, Graham Kelly, Eric Roy and Jill White.

We queue for lunch. There's quite a selection and Scott explains what's what. The clientele lining up today is certainly removed from his usual at the James Cook Hotel in Wellington, but his food isn't. The smorgasbord selection of salads means a big plate.

'Scotty, call for you on 182, Scotty, a call for you on 182.' Ang's soft yet clear voice announces over the PA system.

Comms operator Gloria is out of bed and will take the 1600-midnight shift. With Mat, the base's only other smoker, she enjoys a lunchtime cigarette in the bar – the only place smoking is permitted on base. The pool table in the bar is used every lunch time.

A high-powered telescope by the bar's windows can be used to check on the activities at the sea ice runway. Fewer ski-equipped LC-130 Hercules than usual are lined up at present. The American-run Amundsen-Scott station at the South Pole has now opened for summer and the Hercs are busy shuttling people, supplies and fuel south.

In the mess book corner, a selection of recent New Zealand newspapers, which arrived on Sunday, are in hot demand. Supply officer Bev Gerling enjoys a lunchtime catnap on the couch.

At 1300 it's back to work. Steve makes his daily change of the charts on the seismological helicorders. These charts are analysed for seismic events and the data is e-mailed to the International Seismological Centre in Albuquerque in the United States. Steve's task later this afternoon is to take a set of absolute magnetic readings in the geomagnetic hut.

Sean has made full use of Sylvia's remaining time today. He will continue to make ozone readings with the Dobson spectrometer through the rest of the

A nervous Thingee with summer chef Scott Taylor and chef Scotty.

Addy Atkins and his fan mail.

year on behalf of Sylvia's NIWA team in Wellington. Sean will head to Arrival Heights later to collect some compressed-air samples – a fortnightly task.

In the corridor outside the command centre and the Telecom room Jim has a field radio aerial wound out along the length of the floor Ava has polished this morning. He's making a final check of the HF radio required by Allan Green at Granite Harbour. They should get through to Scott Base on VHF, Channel Three, via the Hoopers Shoulder repeater on Mt Erebus, but the HF radio will be taken as a back-up.

I have my meeting with Senzrep Dave. On entering his office I pass Graham, Jo and Scotty, who are signing out and taking three vehicles to collect the 11 from this afternoon's plane, which is due in half an hour.

Dave catches up on last week's sea ice rescue, which happened while he was in New Zealand. He offers praise, but is more interested to hear of deficiencies. SAR is an ongoing learning process and shortcomings must be converted to improvements. It's early summer and we're still a new team.

He and Alan are happy with the rescheduling of

AFT, with the course for today's incoming 11 beginning this evening.

'There's one more thing,' Dave continues. I'd been expecting it. 'I want that snow-mobile incident report by tomorrow.'

I leave him to his pile of October monthly reports. Work reports are required from most staff every month.

Down in the garage I catch up on Joe and Dennis's assessment of the snow-mobiles. Rachel and Tarn took a trip out on the ice shelf on Sunday and both snow-mobiles broke down. The wrong fuel mix is suspected, but as Joe and Dennis's investigations have proven inconclusive they're sending the heads and pistons out to New Zealand on today's flight for further evaluation. I'll inform Rachel and Tarn when they return.

Thankfully these snow-mobiles aren't required for field events in the next week or two, but all the same, vehicles out of action are a chink in the armour if others break down too. This environment is tough on vehicles.

Rachel, Tarn and the AFT crew arrive home just before 1500, while I'm attending to the toilet buckets and grey-water barrel. I pass on Dave's request for

A passionate farewell for Dan Keller (right) and Sylvia Nichol

the incident report and offer to take tonight's AFT lecture. Tarn will give a hand to fit crampons and run through the prussiking exercise and Rachel will have the evening off.

It's like a railway station down at the entrance to the base. Dressed in full survival gear, today's arrivals look hot on such a warm day. The first-time arrivals must be wondering if everyone gets a welcome like this and whether this really is Antarctica. It's so warm. The afternoon's maximum reaches -5.4°C.

But it's not for the new arrivals that we have assembled. Scotty is about to drive Dan and Sylvia to the plane.

Auckland University zoologist John Macdonald, who's just arrived, has seen all this before. He's a regular visitor to Scott Base and understands the strength of friendships formed down here. Like a homing pigeon, John heads for his quarters in Q Hut – probably no one else has spent more time listening to Q Hut's squeaky floors over the years.

Gazza has painted a big 'See Yaa' sign for the occasion. As the vehicle leaves, almost the entire base is out to wave a passionate farewell.

Ang, who misses the action while attending to the radios, announces that Yvonne and Danny's helicopter will be here in 10 minutes. They grab a

hot drink from the engineering smoko room and go out to the helo pad to wait.

'Brucie, give me a call on 734, Brucie, give me a call on 734 please.' Not only voices are becoming familiar over the PA but also idiosyncratic expressions. Few say please – that has to be Jan. The Maytag washing machine has stopped midway through its cycle and won't restart, so Bruce is called to the rescue.

Ava finishes her day's cleaning down in the engineers' smoko room. It's not too bad today.

Jo's still having problems with the photocopier in the command centre and makes a series of pages for Steve to give her a call. He's not responding.

Scott, who made arrangements with Steve to go cross-country skiing after dinner, knows Steve is out in the geomag hut, so he stops working on Tom's polar tent birthday cake for tomorrow and dials 620, putting him on the PA.

'Aaaaeeeeoooo, Steve's out in the geomag hut, Jo, nic, nic.'

'Aaaaeeeeoooo, nic, nic,' Jo acknowledges.

Today's new arrivals, who have had a cuppa and are receiving their introduction to Scott Base from Graham, must be rather bewildered by this carry-on. Particularly Germans Burkhart Schroeter and

Ludgar Kappen, who are working with Allan Green.

'Now, stop what you are doing and listen up,' blazes across the PA. No one has any doubts with this catch-cry. Mattress Back is having a quiet patch in the shop and he wants the new arrivals to realise the base has a shop. He launches into a hard sell.

At 1700 Mattress Back has the grilles up in the bar. Today's arrivals enjoy a beer while waiting for their personal baggage, which Mat has gone to McMurdo to collect, along with some precious inward mail and the 'guard mail' (official business mail between Scott Base and the office in Christchurch).

Gloria announces that Gentle 11 (American Helicopter) is five minutes out from Scott Base. Alan and Tom, enjoying a pre-dinner Speights, concur that Yvonne and Danny must be returning. Today's weather in the Ferrar must have precluded a landing. Tom heads down to meet the helo.

Dinner tonight is schnitzel and a big selection of vegetables with the option of gravy or creamy herb sauce. Apple pie with custard follows.

It's time for the dishes. Ava reminds those not cleaning their dishes properly that the rinser 'is not a bloody dishwasher'. Gazza and Tim Haskell give a hand with the pots and pans.

Most of the mail in today's bag, sorted into pigeonholes in the command centre, is quickly claimed. I've a large envelope from Liz containing a wad of clippings from local Central Otago newspapers, but they'll have to wait because the AFT lecture starts soon at 1900.

At the same time Scott Base is lining up against McMurdo's Waste Management team at McMurdo's twin-laned 10-pin bowling alley. These alleys are not exactly level and have a habit of guttering many Kiwi attempts. Tonight Scott Base goes down 503 to 402: Addy 97, Bev 107, Graham 106 and Jim 92.

Jacqui, Ava and Ang have squeezed into Toyota T-17 with the bowlers so they can go shopping at McMurdo's 'ship store'. They conclude that Mattress Back has more to offer, so adjourn to the coffee house to wait for the bowls to finish.

Scott, Rachel and Steve Thomas cross-country skiing

Kiwi cargo handlers from McMurdo enjoy an
evening raid of our fridge

Jan attends to Thingee after a night in the bar

Bruce and Rachel join Scott and Steve for a cross-country ski out to the iceberg 7km from Scott Base. With little wind, light clothing can be worn; very different from a month ago. The flagged route to the iceberg leads through the pressure ridges in front of the base and Rachel spies some areas that need further safety flagging – another responsibility for the AFT team. Weddell seals bask in the sun.

Tuesday night is Kiwi night at Scott Base's bar for McMurdo's Kiwis. These nights are not so busy now, as the days of McMurdo hiring Kiwi domestic and kitchen staff have come to an end. An 'American only' employment policy has now been implemented.

But there's a good showing tonight. Wayne Henry's defence force cargo handlers are this summer's regulars and Rangi Pirihi's '03' helicopter contingent of three flight and five service crew make their first visit tonight. Kiwis mountaineers Jon de Vries and John McNamee, and Kiwi fisherwoman Joce Turnbull, all working with American science events, call by.

Joce is fishing for a group investigating antifreeze proteins in fish. Scott Base's fisherwoman, Robyn Holland, has arrived today to fish for John Macdonald's event so they are introduced for the first time.

Thingee and his TVNZ mates recount heroic deeds out on AFT and his presence stamps a real feeling of Kiwiana tonight.

Only three nights after Saturday's aqua party all evidence of the drenching the bar's carpet took has absolutely disappeared, such is the low humidity here. Only thirsts take a drenching tonight.

Scott, back from his ski, is rostered on for the 2200 'mouse round', during which he must check the length of the base. Doors to the outside are to be secure, various switches on or off as required and a check made for fire-safety compliance in plant rooms and workshops. There are many temperature and pressure gauges to check, fuel taps are to be off and vehicles left in the cold have their block heaters plugged into mains power.

Technological advance and the employment of domestic staff have dramatically reduced the duties of the mouse, once known as the housemouse, over the years.

The grille comes down in the bar at 2230 on weeknights. Tonight's guests leave by 2300 and some residents continue with another can or two.

As the sun lowers in the southern sky, casting soft light through the base's windows, the mess is busy with chat and the toaster's timer ticks by. A piece of toast and a cuppa, or a raid of the fridge for a snack, are popular late in the evening. Washed cups and plates stacked in the racks are ready for a rinsing in Ava's rinser, a task attended to before the day's finished.

After a visit to the ablutions and across the squeaky floor it's time to prepare quietly for bed.

Lynette relieves Gloria as communications operator at midnight.

ADRIAN HAYTER: HOUSEMOUSE DUTIES 1965

In his book *The Year of the Quiet Sun* Adrian Hayter, base leader 1964-65, recorded the duties of the 'housemouse':

Usually the housemouse came on duty at reveille and his first job was to clear away after breakfast, wipe the tables down and then wash up everything except the pots, which were the cook's responsibility.

He then went through the base to replace the filled gash (rubbish) paper disposal bags with new ones and empty all gash cans, all of which he then loaded onto a trailer behind a tractor and took away to the rubbish dump in the tide crack beyond the hangar. He then, with a snow vehicle or a clean trailer, collected the snow necessary to top up the snow melters, which are heated tanks built into the buildings and from which the fresh water requirements are drawn.

His next job was to lay the tables for lunch, and again for tea, after which he washed up as usual and then continued on night duty until relieved at the next reveille. In between housemouse duties he did his own particular job at base.

Night duty consisted of tidying up the mess and mopping it out, which was no small task after most social evenings. He also mopped out the ablution block and cleaned the hand basins, and if he was lucky, i.e. if the honey bins (lavatory pans) happened to be full on his tour, he dumped these in the tide crack and replaced with new. (These honey bins were 44-gallon drums cut down to fit under the lavatory seats. Removing them was not as unpleasant as it sounds because the contents froze quickly into a more or less odourless solid.)

The housemouse also carried out a full hourly inspection of the base, looking for fire or anything that might cause a fire, such as clothing left to dry near a heater. His last duties before handing over to his relief were to lay the tables for breakfast and to get the base out of bed at reveille.

Most men, myself included, groused about housemouse duty because it interfered with their normal routine; but once launched we liked it because it did. During the long night watch you could also play whatever music you liked on the record player, if you were lucky. Sometimes others stayed up late playing cards, or a sleepless bleary-eyed monster would come in at any hour to get himself a cup of tea; or there would be such a mess to clear up that you would have little time for anything else.

Adrian Hayter

Adrian operated a system where two shared the housemouse duty each day. Only the cook and the radio operator were excused because of the nature of their duties. This system provided better safety, with two out collecting snow, especially in foul weather, and provided better fire surveillance, with less chance of one mouse falling asleep if on duty all night.

One took the watch until 0100 and cleaned out the mess, then the second, after some sleep, took over until reveille and cleaned out the ablutions.

The housemice would bath and launder the night before their mouse duties. That way they could use as much water as they wished, as it would be they who topped up the snow melters the following day.

Adrian records in his book that he had trouble convincing one man to adopt the system:

'Well, I still don't agree,' said a stubborn one. 'I'm going to do the job on my own.'

'You'll make up your pair like everybody else,' I said, 'and do the job in the way decided.'

'Is that an order?' he asked.

'Yes,' I said, 'that's an order.'

Adrian Hayter died in 1990.

7

FAMS AND FUN

Our operations manual reads: 'Normal working hours are 0800-1700 Monday to Saturday.' Staff are also 'on call at all times'.

The working day complete, some find satisfaction with a night in the bar, one of the parties at Scott Base and McMurdo, or the sports competitions on offer at McMurdo: 10-pin bowling, volleyball, basketball, softball and indoor soccer included. McMurdo now has a climbing wall for the vertically inclined.

Local walks, a cross-country ski or a ski on Scott Base's skifield will take you outdoors. But most want more than that. Most support staff come to Antarctica not for the work or the money but for the place itself. This means getting away from base as much as possible to experience the views, the history and the wildlife.

Trips for recreation or familiarisation, known as 'fams', are permitted provided there's no disruption to work or Scott Base's operation. If possible, fams are scheduled around supporting events or other worthwhile tasks, such as checking fire extinguishers or refuelling refuge huts.

Fams also improve morale and, as a consequence, productivity. Offsetting this, the transport required is a cost and any visit to places such as the Dry Valleys, even if it leaves only footprints, has an impact on the environment.

Scott Base is small enough to give its staff reasonable opportunity. Most of those who spend the whole summer at Scott Base will have been to Cape Evans and Cape Royds for visits to Scott's and Shackleton's historic huts, and will have flown by helicopter to visit Vanda Station or a field event.

Atop Hagglunds H-16, travelling the sea ice to Cape Royds

Mt Erebus from Turtle Rock

Most get to see seals, Adelie penguins and ice caves, and most visit a tourist ship. Priority is given to base-bound staff.

Our American neighbours, because of their numbers, are not so fortunate. But they do enter a ballot for seats on Herc flights to the South Pole. Kiwis seldom get to the Pole these days.

Jo and Peter of ITN require material on the state of the historic huts and New Zealand AHT's efforts to preserve them. They're keen to promote the existence of these monuments to fellow Britons as part of their heritage and hope to encourage funding from home for future preservation work. Our AHT are the caretakers of this heritage.

This season's sea ice, reputed to be the second-heaviest on record, is extremely good. Late November, travelling to Cape Royds via the sea ice can be out of the question – especially with the crack systems off the Barne Glacier and Cape Barne cutting access.

H-16 is packed. Bruce, Jim and Scotty join Jo, Peter, Tim and me.

The flagged route towards Cape Evans is a bit like a main highway by this time of the year, allowing good speed. However, the section adjacent to Turtle Rock slows progress because strong prevailing winds zipping across Hut Point Peninsula nearby have deposited snow on this section, making it very bumpy.

Near the tip of the Erebus Glacier Tongue extending out onto McMurdo Sound we stop to photograph a pod of sunbathing Weddell seals. Open sea ice cracks in summer provide easy access to the water, whereas in winter the seals are forced to gnaw open vital access holes, which continually freeze, with their teeth.

Most of the pups, born six or eight weeks earlier, have grown and are now being weaned. Some have sharp teeth, going by the blood on the snow and the lesions on their mothers' bellies. But the pups

Well fed and content – a Weddell pup with mum

continue to nuzzle for lipid-rich milk, or could it be they're practising their ice-gnawing skills? The results are predictable – bellowing and wrestling more vigorous than is usual for such docile, slug-like creatures.

Beyond the Erebus Glacier Tongue the smoother ice with its well-healed straight-edged cracks poses no problems. The *arête massif* summit of Big Razorback Island appears on our right; like a mountain piercing cloud it protrudes 60m above the sea ice. The Dellbridge Islands on our left are less dramatic.

The first impression one gets of Scott's 1910-13 expedition hut at Cape Evans is its size. This 15m x 7.6m building was home for 25 men.

Leaving H-16 parked on the sea ice we step across benign tide cracks onto Home Beach and approach the locked door. Peter films a group briefing. For the camera I read from the Code of Conduct: 'No more than 12 inside at any time, remove snow and scoria from boots and clothing before entering, no handling of items and definitely no smoking, tilley or gas lamps.'

The cold and darkness are uninviting and it takes time for our eyes to adjust after the brightness outside.

Cold dry conditions and AHT work have preserved the hut very well, but things are not exactly as they were left by Scott's party in 1913.

Shackleton's hut at Cape Royds with an Adelie penguin rookery beyond and the distant Royal Society Range

The Aurora party supporting Shackleton's proposed trans-Antarctic crossing lived in this hut in 1915-17. Shackleton's Endurance party didn't even land, becoming locked in the Weddell Sea's ice, and a two-year epic of survival followed after the *Endurance* sank. This is the expedition where Shackleton made his open-boat trip to South Georgia. With no communications and the *Aurora* also lost, the support party ploughed on, laying depots to the bottom of the Beardmore Glacier as planned. Three died, and seven were rescued in 1917.

The historical tomes of Scott, Wilson, Cherry-Garrard and Priestley, immortalising the 'Heroic Era' (1895-1917), centre on this humble abode at Cape Evans. The rolls of film used by almost four decades of visitors to photograph the many items of interest inside this hut, especially the well-preserved tins and packages of foodstuffs, could go a long way to filling the hut, as ice and snow once did.

After the 'Heroic Era' snow infiltrated the growing nooks and crannies. In 1960-61 Kiwi Les Quartermain and his team began digging out the ice and AHT's preservation work has continued.

During our four-hour visit Peter thoroughly films the interior, using bright halogen lighting for part of it. We empathise with the hut's overpowering mood of tragedy. Jo and Peter are particularly humbled by the experience and speculate on what interest there would be if this monument were to be relocated to Britain.

Tim interviews a few of us for a National Radio documentary; I find it particularly difficult to translate the feelings of this place into words.

Shackleton's hut at Cape Royds, 11km further up the coast, feels much friendlier on two counts. First, once the protective shutters are removed, extra daylight infiltrates larger windows. And secondly, Shackleton survived his Antarctic epics.

The interior of Shackleton's hut

Increasing tourism could pose a threat for these huts. The thousands of people visiting could accelerate the degradation process simply by breathing. Increased ultra-violet (UV) radiation from ozone depletion can also cause damage.

We speculate about encasing the building in a clear vapour-resistant, UV-resistant perspex dome, with a perspex corridor and alcoves inside. Fogging and photo-flash bounce-back would be problems inside. Maybe it would be easier to ban visiting entirely.

We spend a relatively warm evening, camped on the sea ice in three tents pitched beside two locked-in icebergs. These bergs form a spectacular backdrop. The day's maximum has been -8.7°C and the minimum -16.6°C.

Scotty happily attends to dinner, cooking over two kerosene primuses with a sleeping mat propped up to shield the stoves against a very slight breeze.

In these conditions we can comfortably sit outside on wooden food, kitchen or primus boxes and discuss the day's visits. These days, few field parties bother with dehydrated ingredients, favouring frozen whole food. Scotty has packed a generous serving of fresh mushrooms to garnish tonight's rich beef stroganoff, vegetable stir-fry and pasta. Dining at

Fry's cocoa tins in Scott's hut

Top: Cape Royds Adelie penguins. Below left: Our sea ice campsite. Right: Erebus Glacier Tongue ice cave.

below zero, quick eating and little talking are important if you enjoy your food warm. The final scrapings in your bowl become frozen fast.

There is a busy Adelie penguin rookery near Shackleton's hut. Late in November the thousands of birds have completed their battles for pebbles for their nests, on which the females have laid their eggs earlier in the month. The male now contentedly incubates his partner's two eggs while she goes to feed in open water many kilometres to the north. Unneighbourly disputes flare up from time to time. Incubation takes a little more than a month and chicks are brooded for just under another month. Unlike the larger emperors, these smaller birds can breed during summer and migrate north to spend winter on the relatively warmer sea ice.

Returning to Scott Base, we divert to the American field camp Solar Barn, the scene of the SAR three weeks earlier. We observe seals and penguins feeding and moving through the water with far more grace than they can muster on land.

Gracefulness varies on Scott Base's skifield. Once, the Scott Base Ski Club cloth patch was almost as coveted as a silver fern. Wearers then were all required to descend the field's mixed ice and powder slopes with at least one turn in a controlled manner without falling. Today's quick-buck merchants, like Mattress Back, feel commercial gain should outweigh any such tradition and the patches should go on sale to all comers. The debate arises frequently at Scott Base because our patch-crazy neighbours are not officially permitted to ski our field.

An old McMurdo truck, destined for the floor of McMurdo Sound in 1986-87 (a practice New Zealand was guilty of too), has been converted to drive 500m of heavy hemp rope 250m up the eastern slopes of Hut Point Peninsula.

With no more than four on the tow at any time, the queue at the bottom is of little significance and for a couple of hours after dinner you can ski your heart out.

No one makes more of an impact on the field during summer 1994-95 than Addy. The frustrations induced by lumbering along for eight hours a day on a bulldozer are vented on a snowboard. But most of his descents are not of patch-qualifying standard through lack of turns.

We decide to issue a challenge this season with gold, silver and bronze membership. A gold comes

Scott Base skifield during a moderately busy evening

from mastering all three: downhill, telemark on cross-country skis and snowboard, with silver for two pursuits and bronze for one. But getting a look-in on the one board is difficult and only Bruce masters all three by season's end.

Joe valiantly tries for silver membership by attempting to tube the field. Aware of the need for turns, he inserts himself into a large vertically-aligned tube, closes his eyes and proceeds to roll down the hill, with little success. It's the sort of thing Scotty would do.

Scotty's disappointment of summer is missing out on the major prize at McMurdo's fancy dress Halloween Party – a seat in the LC-130 Hercules to South Pole. Scotty goes to extraordinary lengths with impressive improvisation and materials specifically flown down for the creation in order to win the prize. He's confident, but his timing proves less than immaculate. His creation is too cumbersome and hot to perform in all night, so he decides to change in time for the 2130 judging. His mistake. His information sources have failed him on this occasion and the judging commences earlier.

A mad panic ensues. 'Addy, come quick!' The creation is trucked over on the back of T-31. Dressing outside in the cold, he encounters problems with his perspex dome, as his breath condenses on the inside of the cold barrier and he can't reach inside to wipe the fog away. Fully dressed, with lights flashing, bursts of dry-ice smoke and in almost a total whiteout, he has to be led in. Enter the space monster!

The judging has finished. But credit where credit is due and winner JASART Brooks concedes that Scotty's creation is better – but not good enough for him to give up his prize.

Scott Base holds parties on at least a monthly basis. Theme parties are popular and a varied range of costumes has been accumulated over the years.

A toga party is the regular first-up most summers, as it is for us. The Roman soldier outfits are quickly scored for this party by Senzrep Dave and Ron Rodgers, who's down on a visit. The supplies of old sheets take another hammering.

Dave, in his October Senzrep report, records: 'True to form, this group's first party is a toga party. What's the bet the next will be a bad taste or an aqua party?' He's right. An aqua party does follow, but even he couldn't have anticipated January's Culturally Insensitive, Inside Out, Dennis Ham Look-a-like Party in honour of the season's second 'legend'. Even our McMurdo guests scratch their heads over this one.

Scotty the space monster

A Scott Base annual event – the toga party

66

LEO SLATTERY: SCOTT BASE'S 25TH ANNIVERSARY APPLE-PIE INCIDENT

Bob Thomson (RBT), director of the Antarctic Division of the DSIR, was just off to sleep when the door of his bunk-room opened and the light went on. RBT sat up with a jerk, hitting his head on the top bunk and ready to blast the daylights out of the intruder until, quite shocked, he noticed in the doorway the unmistakable figure of the Prime Minister, Robert Muldoon.

Rob was prepared to suffer his bed being apple-pied once, but when it happened a second time he demanded to see the boss. RBT helped make the PM's bed and tucked him in.

The list of VIPs attending Scott Base's 25th anniversary on 20 January 1982 was impressive, despite logistical limitations and an accommodation shortage due to the base's rebuilding programme.

Among the notables were Dr Ian Shearer (Minister for Science), Bruce Beetham (MP), Dr David Kear (Director-General of the DSIR), Dr Trevor Hatherton (Director of the Geophysics Division of the DSIR and IGY leader), Sir J. Holmes Miller (chairman of the RDRC), Sir Edmund Hillary (TAE and first Scott Base leader), Wing Commander Bill Cranfield (TAE RNZAF pilot) and Harry Ayers (TAE field leader), as well as representatives from the United States, Soviet Union, Japan and China.

Weather conditions prevented this deputation visiting the Dry Valleys, but use was made of the radio communications to speak to field parties. Husky-pulled sledge rides were popular.

The flags of 13 consecutive Antarctic Treaty nations flew in front of Scott Base. A simple flag ceremony, almost identical to that of 1957, involved Sir Edmund lowering the old flag and Scott Base's youngest member, 18-year-old student Kathleen Smith, raising a new flag to herald the commencement of the new era.

Cocktails, a sumptuous buffet dinner and many

Leo Slattery with PM Rob Muldoon

speeches followed. The official part of the evening concluded with Trevor Hatherton presenting the PM with a specially made tie embroidered with the words: 'One Way – My Way'. Celebrations continued, long and arduous.

When the boarding passes were handed out at Williams Field in readiness for the flight home, an American NSFA official enquired:

'Muldoon?'

Rob, disguised behind dark sunglasses and with a wry smile, dutifully put up his hand.

The culprits who perpetrated the apple-pieing of the PM's bed were duly brought to account and shortlisted for an early flight home. They shall remain nameless.

[Leo Slattery is one of only eight people who have done three winters at Scott Base. For the years 1979-80, 1981-82 and 1984-85 he was the base's postmaster, and winter-over officer in charge for the latter two.]

From top left: Scotty and *Dissotichus mawsoni* for the Senzrep dinner; my delivery of the royal toast at Senzrep dinner; Scotty and Scott's wonderful Christmas feast; Scully (Cullum Boleyn) is an able dishwasher.

Formal dining is enjoyed with the Senzrep dinner. On 3 December we dine out Dave Geddes and dine in NZAP science liaison officer Malcolm Macfarlane, who's the Senzrep for the second half of summer. The menu includes fresh *Dissotichus mawsoni*, or Antarctic cod, caught by John Macdonald's team. Recreational fishing isn't permitted, but when science needs only organs and blood, the flesh is sent to the kitchen.

Christmas Day is the other summer occasion for which we dress in our best. The day starts with the managers' brunch. With my winter management role

approaching, Alan, Graham, John and Malcolm invite me to assist. Apart from Scott and Scotty, the rest of the team enjoy a leisurely start to the day, following last night's engineers' Mexican banquet.

Managers' brunch at 1000 offers pancakes, syrup and cream; a selection of fresh fruits; bacon, eggs, tomatoes and hash browns; champagne or juice and coffee. Service is of Kiwi Host standard.

To remind ourselves we're here to support science, a Scott Base Christmas regular is Elevenses at Einstein's or 'a little something' (à la A.A. Milne) up in the Hatherton Laboratory. Sean and Steve pour a glass or two of 'seismic white' or 'ionospheric red'. Old seismic charts on the walls, white coats, subdued light and the confined office space add to the seedy ambience. Sean wears safety glasses and drinks from his best beaker.

With this diversion, Rachel and Scully sneak out and set up two black-painted particle-board orca shark fins in a melt pool in front of the base.

'Hey, look at that out there!'

By 1300 Scotty is in need of a break from the kitchen so Santa makes his scheduled visit with a sack of 32 $5 gifts – one for everyone on base today.

Ava, Jan, Jacqui and many others help Scott and Scotty in the kitchen. The time-management skills and efficiency of our culinary masters amazes.

At 1500, with everyone showered and dressed, every dish is at the right temperature and every item of food of optimum texture. This is very much the pinnacle for our chefs this summer.

The day continues in relaxed mode and tomorrow, Boxing Day, we will burn off those extra calories on the skifield.

The other pinnacle reached this summer is attained by Rachel and Tom on a JASART training trip when they climb to the highest point of the Royal Society Mountains, Mt Lister (4025m). In this latitude's rarefied air this equates to an altitude closer to 5000m nearer the Equator, which is close to requiring acclimatisation. McMurdo JASART members Mike and Steve, both experienced at altitude, set a very slow pace to the summit. Headaches abound and at the end of the exercise it is agreed that SAR this high would be more than a challenge.

New Year's Day proves not too much of a headache for Addy, Alan, Dave Campbell, Dave Mitchell, Rachel, Scott, Scotty and Steve. They climb Mt Aurora on Black Island.

Rudolph (Ruth Golombok) hauls Santa's (Scotty) sledge with Rachel, Dawn-Lee Hartley and Colin Harris

8

THE TOURIST SEASON ENDS

The first groups disembark from the cumbersome Mil-8. This Russian helicopter isn't pretty, nor is the ship it has flown from. The *Kapitan Khlebnikov*, moored against the sea ice further out in McMurdo Sound, is a converted Russian icebreaker that lacks the sleeker lines of other tourist vessels visiting Antarctica. But it's delivering the goods. It has bashed its way through this season's extra-heavy sea ice conditions for three visits and its passengers have been able to visit us each time.

Ice-strengthened ships *Bremen* and MV *Akademic Shokalski* couldn't get their passengers far enough into McMurdo Sound for visits to Scott Base this season.

On 21 February, five days before the summer's last LC-130 Hercules flies out from Williams Field, we entertain the *Kapitan Khlebnikov*'s final visit. A weather deterioration is forecast but is holding off and it's very warm – a +1.3°C maximum is recorded today. Only two Christchurch staff, Gill and NZAP personnel officer Jenny Prier, remain to help the winter team host the visit of this predominantly Australian contingent.

Greg Mortimer's leathery, weather-beaten face marks him out from the group, as does his blue mountain jacket among the red-issue jackets. An Australian mountaineer and adventurer, Greg has visited Antarctica often since 1978, initially as a geologist, then on private expeditions. He's the tour leader of this 'Quark Expeditions' visit. He marshals his charges and speaks to the helicopter and ship via his hand-held radio.

They enter Scott Base. There is a mixed response to the sight of a litter-box sporting some genuine-looking (used) cat litter. Tiddles, Scott Base's leg-

Left: Scotty on board the *Kapitan Khlebnikov* during its second 1994-95 summer visit.
Right: Jim decommissions Mt J.J. Thompson's VHF repeater at the end of summer.

endary cat, is very shy. I wonder if our visitors' thoughts stretch back to on-ship lectures that may have referred to the Madrid Protocol precluding all exotic animals from Antarctica.

In under an hour each group of 10 is treated to an explanation of the Hatherton Laboratory, a full inspection of all living quarters, a cuppa and scones, a rummage through the shop's dwindling stocks and, for the very keen, a look in the workshop areas. The Scott Base cachet stamps prove popular, so friends and family back home can receive Antarctic mail.

Our visitors are then transported to McMurdo, courtesy of our fleet, for a visit that includes Scott's Discovery hut. Their hulking Mil-8 returns them to the boat, presently moving back down the sound. By late this evening the last will be returning from a visit to the Taylor Valley.

Many of the visitors envy our lot, but the envy is reciprocated, as they are experiencing the joys of cruising on the southern oceans. Five of our team – Dave, Jan, Jim, Joe and Tom – take a Mil-8 backflight and enjoy an hour's visit on board the ship.

Tourist visits to Antarctic bases can be considered a kind of audit – the public's opportunity to see where their tax dollars are going and, more important, how environmentally 'clean' our operations are. Most tourists visiting Antarctica have high conservation awareness. Some are well known and respected in society, and their impressions easily become public.

The visitors abide by strict guidelines. Those on the *Kapitan Khlebnikov* were not permitted to eat, smoke, litter or relieve themselves on shore beyond the bounds of the national bases. Government representatives join each tourist cruise to keep an eye on proceedings.

Winter-over staff joke: 'Summer support staff are tourists too.'

With assignments complete, Dan, Dennis and Tails return home before Christmas. But the main

Journalist Keith Lyons photographs another visitor – a snail that arrived in the lettuces.

summer exodus begins with Gazza, Rachel and Scully's departure on 22 January.

Four months together in an environment such as this forms strong bonds of friendship and today's mixed-gender society adds an extra dimension to this friendship.

During the summer of 1969-70 Pam Young joined her husband Euan's science event as an assistant, becoming the first woman to work on New Zealand's programme. In 1978-79, science officer Thelma Rodgers became the first woman to winterover at Scott Base.

The degree of bonding during summer 1994-95 becomes apparent during a trial run of Gazza's approaching wedding – albeit in the absence of his Spanish fiancée. Gazza met Rosario in Spain while setting up New Zealand's exhibit at Expo '92 in Seville. The trial run is planned for the eve of his departure.

Mattress Back plays Rosario and a full ceremony is planned, with roles allocated and no detail spared. The only point out of order is that Rosario joins Gazza for a seedy stag night at McMurdo.

Our domestic team and bridesmaids Jan, Ava and Jacqui dress in their best black plastic rubbish-bag dresses with pink rubber washing gloves. Improvisation is required for flowers, with a fresh Goldilocks dish-scourer buttonhole spray and a dish-scrubber posy. Best man Scully and groomsmen Mat and Tom contrast in white disposable protective suits.

PETER 'JOCK' WALTON: COVERT HOSPITALITY

I took one of the huskies (or rather it dragged me) for a walk up Crater Hill and, sitting on top, I gawked at the only half decent auroral display we'd had all winter. I felt insignificant yet comfortable – if this is the edge of the world I'm still on it. Looking south, my eyes fixed on Minna Bluff and I wondered what it must be like to trudge at a snail's pace across 700km of Ross Ice Shelf before hauling uphill to the South Pole for almost another 700.

In a few months those guys up at Cape Evans will be doing that.

Those guys were treated by officialdom as the scourge of Antarctica. A non-governmental organisation (NGO) and a private expedition – the first unofficial winter-over team on Ross Island. Officialdom thought of them only as trouble as it was inevitable that they would get into trouble.

Those guys were the 'In the Footsteps of Scott' expedition: Britons Robert Swan, Roger Mear, Mike Stroud and John Tolson and Canadian Gareth Wood. The official line was for us to keep our distance.

Three – Robert, Mike and Gareth – had just completed the winter trip to Cape Crozier, as Wilson, Bowers and Cherry-Garrard had in 1911. That made us less sceptical.

They arrived at the end of summer (early 1985) and established base beside Scott's hut at Cape Evans. Now into late winter, they had visited on several previous occasions and had also stayed at McMurdo.

We were mostly glad to see them – new faces and a different point of view – although on odd occasions some were heard to remark 'What? They're here again! I thought they're supposed to be self-sufficient.'

They may have lost a little credibility staying at Scott Base and McMurdo, but there was a fair amount of mutual co-operation.

I can only remember one occasion when they asked for help. When Gareth's radio mast had blown down for about the 20th time timber was requested and was duly sneaked out – under our OIC Leo's nose.

The 100mm x 100mm oregon beams were scored from McMurdo's dump, to which we made a rubbish run every Saturday. So the Americans unknowingly supported the Footsteps expedition.

We were well received on our visits to their hut at Cape Evans. Robert, the historian, gave a great tour of Scott's hut. They must have got sick of having so many visits during the end of winter, disrupting their preparations for the trip to the Pole. Nevertheless, and despite their own personal conflicts, the hospitality they extended was unstinting.

We were home at the end of winter 1985 before Robert, Roger and Gareth set off. The news came through on 11 January 1986 that they reached the Pole, and unfortunately the same day their ship *Southern Quest* had sunk. They requested official assistance.

The political ramifications of having an NGO at close quarters were again felt at Scott Base the following summer, when Greenpeace moved in at Cape Evans.

When I return at Winfly 1995, a decade later, I can't believe that NZAP is supporting a Greenpeace visit this coming summer. The environmental group is returning to monitor any environmental impact from its 1987-92 occupation. How attitudes have changed.

[Jock Walton, a carpenter, was selected for summer 1984-85, and was invited to stay on for winter 1985. He returned at Winfly 1995 and stayed until early summer.]

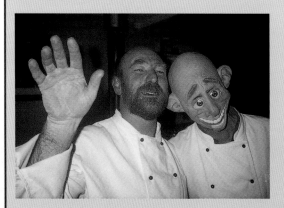

Jock Walton with Richard Struthers, 1995

Coloured socks and a large lime green bow tie add a splash of dash, as does some handiwork with a black marker pen drawing on buttons and pockets.

Parents are in attendance, not to mention flower girl Steve and page boy Addy, complete with carrot rings.

'Father' Scott officiates with a simple service in the Scott Base bar and a warmish day allows photographs to be taken outside in front of the base. The bride and groom look splendid.

The wedding breakfast is a grand affair with a succession of speeches, which go on, and on, and on. Their tenor changes from bawdy and hilarious to lachrymose, lump-in-throat stuff – emotive tributes to friendship, to effort during the season, to a beautiful place and to a truly family-like team.

Scott departs on 29 January with Jacqui, Lynette and Steve. Mechanical malfunction delays departure until 0130, yet most of Scott Base stays up until they leave. Scott leaves a note. It reads:

To all you wonderful bastards and bastesses who inhabited my life for the last four months.

I can't vocalise goodbyes (I tend to get something in my eyes – dust perhaps). It's only been four months that I've known you all, but feels like four years – is that good or bad? But you've left me with a great feeling of belonging. As I contemplate leaving, I feel like someone's ripping out my heart with a pair of John's pliers. It's taken such a short time to build a beautiful family, seems such a shame to tear it apart. I love talking to, working with and cooking for you all. Thanks for eating my food, listening to my garbage and taking my crap. I'll leave you with a Richard Bach poem:

The bond that links your true family
is not one of blood but of respect
and joy in each other's life.
Rarely do members of one family grow
up under the same roof

Thanks to my family, come see me,
Love, Scott.

The bride and groom, Mattress Back and Gazza (Gary Smith)

Dust continues to get in people's eyes during the rest of summer.

Before too many depart, the winter crew make use of appropriate staff as a fire crew so we can get our winter-over team photograph.

Our morning suits arrive from Munns Suit Hire in Christchurch and we have about a week in which to get the photo. We look rather dapper in penguin attire, and Sorrel boots add an extra dimension.

Jan looks rather dapper too. There have been suggestions that she should wear a red dress, which photographically would have looked good, but in terms of being part of a team, Jan's penguin attire is more meaningful.

We make good use of the suits. Scotty arranges for a table to be set in the centre of McMurdo's galley for us to dine out. We look like fish out of water, surrounded by the Americans in their usual dowdy-looking work garb, and we elicit predictable comments: 'Those god-damn crazy Kiwis, what'll they do next?'

We're even invited to visit the *Richard Mathieson*, a fuel tanker, and the *Polar Sea*, an ice-breaker. The ice-breaker's captain shows us around and there are plenty of opportunities for team photo shots.

I have a photo in mind – taken in evening light, which adds texture to the pressure ridge's snow. The team exercises patience and the third time we dress

The 1995 winter-over team boarding the *Richard Mathieson*: Warren, John, Tom, Dave, Sean, Joe, Jan, Jim, Bruce and Scotty

up, Henri Kasper, one of the last summer science event staff, shoots the magic shot. Munns can have their suits back.

One big job before all the summer staff leave is the annual ship off-load early in February. When the sea ice is at its most vulnerable, later in summer, the *Richard Mathieson* and container ship MV *Green Wave* deliver the bulk of our requirements. Their next visit will be a year later.

The *Polar Sea* and its companion United States Coast Guard ice-breaker, the *Polar Star*, remain in the neighbourhood to assist. This season's heavier ice necessitates their cutting a 15km channel into Winter Quarters Bay as well as a decent-sized turning bay.

The off-loading of the MV *Green Wave* is delayed 24 hours as the container lashings have been frozen solid. Eventually we receive our seven containers packed with frozen and dry food, pallets of beer and building materials, and spares for the next 12 months. We also receive three pre-built buildings: a dangerous-goods store, a pumphouse and a wet lab, as well as a new D6 bulldozer.

Human chains can move large quantities quickly so all hands are required to unpack. A nippy wind keeps us honest. Six containers of retrograde are loaded for Lyttelton.

The ice-breakers arrived earlier than usual this season to assist the Italian ship *Italica* position itself close to Cape Roberts to off-load drilling project materials in preparation for the forthcoming multinational Cape Roberts Project.

While they're waiting for shipping operations to be completed the ice-breakers offer assistance to both programmes. We can do with more fuel at our Cape Bird Hut, so 12 44-gallon (208-litre) drums of JP-8 are loaded aboard the *Polar Star*, to be flown ashore at Cape Bird. Scotty and I go to off-load.

We discover that most flight crew must be smaller than us as we squeeze into flotation flight suits on Scott Base's helo pad. We then board the *Polar Star*'s elegant Dauphine helicopter, itself equipped with flotation equipment. The pilot proceeds to instruct us on emergency disembarking in the event that we have to ditch into the sea. 'If bailing out, always keep a hold on that handle,' he yells, and points to the handle above the door. 'That'll be your point of reference so you'll know which way's out.' Nice thought.

In keeping with its sleek looks, the Dauphine flies smoothly and quietly compared with a Huey or an Iroquois. With no need to hug the land, we fix on a direct line to the *Polar Sea*, 12km off Cape Bird.

During recent weeks a huge iceberg has moved across the north of Ross Island and its progress is being plotted by satellite photos at Mac Ops weather centre. We get to appreciate its enormity when flying over it – it's about 10km long and 3-4km wide in places.

This berg broke off the Ross Ice Shelf east of the island and has moved around our western vicinity. It's now positioned off Cape Royds. Penguin workers at Cape Bird observed it moving past a week or two back – at one stage neither end was easily seen. It's amazing that tides and wind can move such a mass, but by Antarctic standards this is not a big one.

Cape Bird is a wonderful place at this time of year and we savour the sound of sea washing onto a stony beach; Scott Base is still locked in with frozen sea ice.

The drums are flown one at a time, unloaded from a cargo net, and the net is then carried down the beach to a pick-up point. We tried two drums on the first flight but they proved too heavy. The weight of flotation equipment reduces the helicopter's lifting ability.

We don't mind the drums coming in one at a time. It gives us extra time at Cape Bird, and two or three round trips out to the *Polar Star* each as we take turns. The task complete, the pilot, realising we're enjoying our day out, flies two crew from the ship back to McMurdo before he returns for us.

The two hours spent sitting on the beach are beautiful. Only a slight breeze blows and the temperature is close to a balmy zero.

Young moulting Adelies balance clumsily on lumps of brash ice, stranded at the water line as they wait for a feed from parents. Their urge for independence is evident as they make tentative splashings, at least getting their feet wet.

There are no sandflies here: the only threat is from Antarctic skuas, which dive-bomb us if we venture

The resupply ship MV *Green Wave* in Winter Quarters Bay about to load

The Dauphine delivering fuel to Cape Bird Hut

A moment of magic during my year on ice – sitting with Adelies beside open water on Cape Bird's beach

anywhere near their territories and chicks. Predatory skuas live on dead and weak Adelie chicks.

There's a relaxed feeling at this 'Côte d'Azur' of Ross Island. Two or three days here, in lieu of the week's rest and recreation leave our McMurdo neighbours get in New Zealand before winter, would be great.

The departure of summer staff can be hard on winter-over members. We're entering a new phase of uncertainty with winter upon us. In a few weeks, after the last plane has departed from Williams Field, nothing will land until Winfly in August. Some have openly admitted a slight temptation to jump ship. But each knows that the experience and acceptance by the rest of the team that has built up during four months would be difficult to replace. We're committed to completing the assignment.

At about 0500 on 26 February Scotty is the only one from Scott Base standing with a group on Observation Hill. He videos the final LC-130 Herc departure for the summer of 1994-95.

9

ESTABLISHING A ROUTINE

One passenger on the *Kapitan Khlebnikov*'s first visit to Scott Base in January is Wally Herbert, a well-known polar worker and traveller who has spent over 13 years in either Antarctica or the Arctic. Wally, who worked with New Zealand's programme during the early 1960s, is best known for making the first dog-sled crossing of the Arctic, about 6000km, in 1968-69.

Wally was pretty experienced at working in a team and shared his thoughts in Nigel Gifford's book *Expeditions & Exploration*:

'Now when you're right out in the middle of the Arctic and you've been on the move for, say, eight months, and you're at a point called The Pole of Inaccessibility, which is the point furthest from land in any direction, you have come to know the other men pretty well. In fact you totally rely on each other socially. It's now that you have to start to use your imagination; and it's worth mentioning that there is no point in having someone along who has a great repertoire of jokes, which might last for about a year and a half, because no man is that bloody clever! So you must have men that are able to improvise, men that have a lively intellect, and an interest in what is to be seen around; a great sense of humour is important too, and an ability to create things to say. You cannot just depend on a repertoire of stories.'

'Improvisation', 'lively intellect', 'a sense of humour' and 'creativity' – how about a garden gnome? Bruce the Gnome, who mysteriously went miss-ing from my garden in Clyde a month before I flew south, re-appears at the base of the flagpole on 7 October in time for handover. He receives only sporadic attention throughout summer, though nothing as common as 'gnome-napping'.

Bruce's presence in the bar, sitting on the piano, usually goes unnoticed. For the most part, attention is focused on him only when he crushes cans. A line-up of aluminium cans across the carpeted floor is no problem for an 11kg smiling concrete gnome. (The same can't be said for steel juice cans.) MPs visiting Scott Base enjoy him and visitors from McMurdo enjoy him. However, some of the *Kapitan Khlebnikov*'s Russian crew can't relate to Bruce. Their dead-pan faces contrast with his.

Bruce features at a bad-taste Irish party as Bruce the Blarney Gnome. People lip-smack his concrete derriere then make a wish – an act no easier than kissing the Blarney Stone in Ireland. Gymnastic effort is required to hold on to a dumb-bell bar, lean right back and reach up under Bruce, who is set up on a weights rack.

Bruce the Gnome and friends

The base gnome is also resplendent in tux and sunglasses for the team's winter-over photograph.

But none of the dastardly things that happen to Bruce through the summer compares with what happens during the week leading up to the official winter handover. Two sequences of Polaroid shots almost convince me of gnomic demise. Firstly, a crushing under the blade of the new D6 bulldozer. Then, a very good sequence showing a flying gnome splashing into the sea through the now large hole in the sea ice where the seawater intake pipe hangs. But the team know better than to mess with a gnome belonging to the about-to-become boss. When Malcolm lowers the summer flag at 1630 on 9 February and I raise the new one for winter, Bruce is, once again, sitting at the base of the flagpole. This time he's encased in a core of ice.

With our new flag flying, new routines are implemented. During past weeks we've accommodated fewer people on base and are enjoying the extra space – especially having a whole bedroom each. A mess with nine dining tables has been converted to a friendlier place with just four tables, allowing room in the TV corner for a large six-seater couch.

For most, their tasks continue on from summer but I move from the freedom of the field to the confines of the base. My duties now include monitoring meteorological, geomagnetic and seismic programmes, administration, running the shop and bar plus management duties. I move into the office Malcolm has vacated.

My team has demonstrated a high degree of conscientiousness and is generally harmonious so I feel confident that my preferred style of consensus leadership will work.

All groups need ground rules so we all discuss a list of issues that will affect our lives, particularly those outside work, involving rosters, social activities and visitors on base.

A regular personal routine of working, eating, sleeping and exercise is important, and is left pretty much to each individual to take care of. This accommodates personal preferences and allows a sense of self-determination.

Scotty's video clip of this morning's departing LC-130 Hercules is ready to play when I return from taking the 0900 daily met obs. These observations have been e-mailed to numerous receivers in New

Left: Making 0900 daily met obs at Stevenson screen. Right: Tom flagging the route to Arrival Heights.

THELMA RODGERS: THREE HUNDRED VISITORS IN ELEGANT DRESS

The end of the summer at Scott Base came suddenly in early February. One moment the base was noisy and bursting at the seams with people and projects around the clock in the perpetual daylight of the Antarctic summer; the next it was empty and echoing as the winter-over team of 12 were left to take up their winter routines.

With the departure of the summer people the Antarctic seemed to come closer; there was a sense of exposure that was both exhilarating and threatening. It was a time to whittle back the exuberant activity of the summer to an underlying structure of necessary routine to keep at bay the encroaching immensity of cold and dark that was the Antarctic winter.

For now the sun began to dip behind the mountains and each day for the next two months the daylight hours would progressively shorten by some 25 minutes until in late April, when the sun would finally set, to remain below the horizon for four months of winter.

Yet while light lasted it was a magic time at Scott Base, for the Antarctic wildlife came visiting.

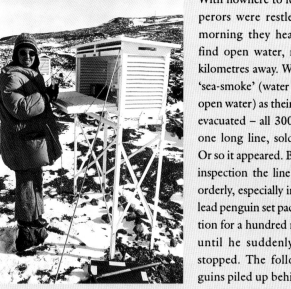

Thelma Rodgers

The sea ice immediately in front of the base had appeared to be an extension of the land: dangerous with tidal crack and the occasional saltwater-melt pool, but relatively solid and distinctly unlike water.

So with great excitement on the last morning in February we woke to find the sea ice had 'broken out' in the night, revealing the prime seashore location of Scott Base for the first time.

Out in the water among the plates of floating ice cruised the occasional whale – orca and greys – in pursuit of the seals and the 300 or more emperor penguins that congregated in large and noisy groups along the icy beach of the ice shelf, just a couple of hundred metres from the base.

The emperors were juveniles, not yet ready to join the mating scene at Cape Crozier, and were the object of many photographic expeditions from the base. A human visitor cautiously approaching a group on bended knees would be greeted with warbles of welcome to this strange new penguin, and the incongruity of their elegant dress and their waddling gait and curious antics never failed to enchant and amuse.

But as the light became lower the weather rapidly became colder and within a few weeks the sea was again frozen. With nowhere to feed, the emperors were restless and one morning they headed out to find open water, now several kilometres away. With only the 'sea-smoke' (water vapour over open water) as their guide, they evacuated – all 300 of them in one long line, soldier fashion. Or so it appeared. But on closer inspection the line was not so orderly, especially in front. The lead penguin set pace and direction for a hundred metres or so until he suddenly tired and stopped. The following penguins piled up behind him like a comedy routine from the silent movies, until one from further back would push through and take the lead, only to be chased indignantly by the original leader.

The traces of their zig-zag progression remained on the ice for many days until finally obliterated by blizzards and the encroaching dark.

[Thelma Rodgers was the first woman to winter over at Scott Base during 1978-79 and made three other summer visits as part of her technician's role with the Geophysics Division of the DSIR. Today she is an architect in Auckland.]

Top: John and Tom visiting the ice fall crevasse (note Tom climbing the wall before winter has even started). Below, left: A fortnightly fire drill. Below, right: Jan undertakes a CPR refresher course.

Zealand and faxed to Kelly Tarlton's Antarctic Encounter in Auckland. Visitors there will, in moments, be reading that it's only -12.6°C here, and that yesterday's maximum wind gust was only 16 knots. No doubt more dramatic climatic measurements are expected.

Bruce and Jim are also up so they take a seat. Scotty plays his video tape. The rest can see it later when they get up.

The excitement at winter's arrival now overwhelms any momentary lapses of faith. With the quietness around this place now one does have more time to reflect on the absence of loved ones. But still, they're only a phone call away.

Communications have altered the winter experience. It could be argued that Antarctica has moved from isolation to remoteness. Scott and Shackleton, without contact with the outside world, could have been on a different planet. Today, we receive daily e-mail news and Internet bulletins, and the world is within phone or fax contact 24 hours a day.

Any thoughts of not seeing anyone outside Ross Island for six months are negated almost immediately when the phone rings. From the tone of the ring it's an external call.

It is the crew of the MV *Greenpeace* are phoning via satellite from less than 20km away. They are sitting at the ice edge in McMurdo Sound but are not willing to enter the shipping channel into Winter Quarters Bay as it's freezing over. They have asked that we come up on HF radio on 5400kHz in an hour's time.

Greenpeace is investigating Japanese 'scientific' whaling activities south of the Antarctic Circle at a latitude of 60°S, the region where the Antarctic Treaty's protective legislation applies. MV *Greenpeace* has caught up with a Japanese factory ship and its two catcher craft. Evidence has been recorded and, in retaliation, MV *Greenpeace* has been chased away by one of the catchers, fleeing south into McMurdo Sound for refuge.

Bruce, Dave and I drive up onto Hut Point Peninsula overlooking the sound where MV *Greenpeace* is stationary at the ice edge with the catcher boat standing not too far off.

MV *Greenpeace* keeps in touch and we invite the crew to visit the base. They are keen but an intervening storm changes all that. For 24 hours our attempts to contact them go unanswered.

Eventually we receive a fax. The storm has allowed them to escape the attentions of the Japanese boat by sheltering behind the big iceberg that Scotty and I flew over earlier in the month. After they shut everything down, including communications, the Japanese lost contact and moved off.

Ten days later another fax. The Japanese flotilla has again been sighted, 240km north-east of Ross Island, and MV *Greenpeace* has been chased again. They're now well away, near the Balleny Islands, heading for Hobart.

Throughout this episode, especially when the MV *Greenpeace* fails to respond to our calls, I reflect on how we would respond to a Mayday from a rammed and sinking ship.

During winter, without air support and with travel restricted to a selection of destinations, JASART scenarios become limited.

Only Tom and I remain from the primary summer team, and with Joe, we're members of the winter team. We continue training with the Americans on a twice-monthly basis, concentrating on finding missing people and vehicles in the dark and cold.

Travelling on sea ice, once it's strong enough again in April-May, is permitted only occasionally. We shouldn't have any problems this winter.

 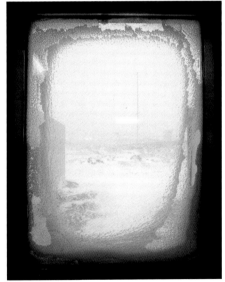

The cold, cold world outside our windows

McMurdo Station in May twilight (top) and the station in midwinter's darkness (below)

10

THE MCMURDO FACTOR

Many Kiwis describe their experience at Scott Base as being both Antarctic and American, such is the influence of our neighbouring metropolis.

Some say McMurdo Station could double as an Alaskan oil-drilling town, and some even go as far as labelling it a bygone American 'frontier town'. The station has witnessed a continuous 'add-on' building programme since IGY in 1957-58 and the decision to continue supporting Antarctic science. It has now become too big for complete replacement. Having more than one controlling organisation has added to the seemingly haphazard nature of the station's evolution.

It accommodates the work and living needs of a summer population of over 1000 and exudes a different persona from the ordered Scott Base.

The National Science Foundation (NSF) has overall responsibility for the American programme, with support from the Naval Support Force Antarctica (NSFA) and Antarctic Support Associates (ASA). The navy has backed the McMurdo operation as Operation Deep Freeze for 40 years and is now progressively handing over to ASA, the organisation that won the support contract.

McMurdo's buildings vary in size, shape and colour. Distinguishing features of the town are its power

Winter Quarters Bay with the Discovery Hut, McMurdo Station and Observation Hill

Images of 'Mactown': Mac Ops, Chapel of the Snows, orange pick-up trucks and many overhead cables

and telephone cables, ground-level heated ducting carrying water and sewage, and dozens of coloured-code waste receptacles for thorough waste separations and collection.

McMurdo is busy during summer, with much of the town's action centring on the massive Crary Science Laboratory. This recently-constructed three-phase building is the station's jewel in the crown. It houses state-of-the-art facilities for all facets of science.

Life is always evident at McMurdo, with the pervading smell of fuels and chimneys emitting plumes of smoke. Orange-painted left-hand-drive pick-up trucks, streaked with dust and dirt, prowl the streets while workers attend to a multitude of tasks. Helicopters supporting events in the field depart and arrive on a regular basis down at the helo pad.

At meal times the streets swarm as red- and green-jacketed citizens head to the 'queen bee' of the town's buildings, '155', which houses the 'galley'. They take care to avoid icy patches and wind-glazed snow. Compacted snow on the steps leading into buildings is a hazard, and most seasons bones are broken. Venturing from building to building can be tough in bad weather. McMurdo doesn't enjoy Scott base's link-way corridors.

McMurdo's population is highly segregated, particularly during summer when three groups form. ASA civilians form one group, with many of them returning season after season; NSFA personnel on 'tours of duty' form the second group; and the summer science fraternity is the third.

ASA and NSFA dominate the town culture, one that is becoming less reliant on booze as the 'frontier town' label recedes. Many say this is attributable to women now making up a quarter of the population.

A gulf exists between the support and science fraternities (the latter colloquially referred to as 'beakers'). Support staff generally have little interest in science and find it difficult to relate to 'nerdy' types and their arcane projects.

With funding for science now partially based on previous results, scientists are under pressure to perform and this means making full use of their Antarctic time. Social interaction and courtesies are often dispensed with as a result and sometimes the expectations placed upon the support staff can be unreasonable. Scott Base's comparatively small population essentially negates this problem.

Scott Base makes use of McMurdo's facilities summer and winter: medical and dental services, free haircuts at the barber's shop, a live radio station and two television channels. There are sports competitions, a ship store, a book and video library, hobbies' huts, gymnasiums for both weights and aerobics, two bars and a coffee house. Waste Management offers Skua Central (named after the predatory bird), a recycling centre for a whole spectrum of items.

Working hard and playing hard: regular maintenance of insulated ducting (left); celebrating Halloween

Spiritual solace is offered with Catholic, Protestant and Jewish services at the Chapel of the Snows; a stained-glass image of a penguin sits over the altar.

The large populations, busy work schedules and Scott Base's small size limit social interaction between McMurdo and Scott Base staff during summer, but winter is different.

Town manager at McMurdo for winter, Al Martin, invites John and me to their first, and subsequent, weekly town meetings. This provides the official and more relaxed link between bases during winter, with the aim of uniting us as the 'Ross Island Society'.

This winter 244 citizens remain at McMurdo: three with NSF, 29 with NSFA, 212 with ASA.

NSFA runs Morale, Welfare and Recreation (MWR), which looks after the ship store, bars and all sport and recreational activities. MWR still employs Kiwis. This year Rod (Rocket) Withers, Nell Boche, Brendan (Slop) McKendry and Ray Smith winter over with MWR.

Al invites me to speak at the first 'all hands' meeting, which most of the town is expected to attend. This is the chance to introduce Scott Base and extend a conditional invitation for Thursday nights.

Some of McMurdo's heavier drinkers regard Scott Base only as Ross Island's third bar and a place where the greenback goes further. But unlike the two bars

in McMurdo, our bar is part of our personal living space and this year we are not really interested in running a watering hole.

'Scott Base doesn't have a dependence on alcohol this winter,' is my opening statement with respect to Thursday nights. 'On Thursday nights, if you want to come over for a coffee, a read or a chat, then you're most welcome.'

This statement elicits little reaction at the meeting, but as the months progress it becomes evident our niche market has been successfully targeted. Our convivial Thursday nights of 10-15 for dinner, then others arriving later for a poke around the shop and then a beer or a coffee are pleasant evenings indeed. The bar-grilles stay up all winter and no one ever needs the hint to go home. It is only near winter's end that I hear of a few 'hard men' branding Scott Base staff as teetotallers. Wrong.

'Come and visit us at Black Island,' says information systems manager Jeff Smith. He's heading out to work at the satellite communications station for two weeks.

Late March remains very settled with a large stationary anticyclone sitting over the Polar Plateau. It sends an outflow of dry, cold glacial air our way and we hit -40°C for our first time.

Sunsets are – or maybe it's just our imagination – becoming more dramatic: 'Just one more shot.'

As far as the eye can see north, McMurdo Sound has totally frozen over now.

Early in April, with air pressures still above 1000 hectopascals, Dave, Jan, John, Sean and I pack H-26 and head to Black Island on a fam trip. I look forward to the opportunity to photograph something new.

The 96km journey to the station follows a heavily flagged route across the Ross Ice Shelf. Our winter JASART has made three trips to complete the flagging of this route, which is used throughout winter's darkness. Our Hagglunds bumps across the sastrugi (ridges of wind-toughed snow) trailing a plume of snow.

Halfway, at the gap between Black and White islands, we make the usual hourly radio contact with Scott Base, this time checking our HF set. We're entering a VHF blackout zone south of the island where we're out of 'line of sight' of Scott Base's Crater Hill repeater, the only one kept up in winter.

Fresh winds blowing through the gap mean we don't linger while rolling up our HF radio aerial. Rougher sastrugi behind the island hint of stronger winds in this area. The afternoon cloud eventually dissipates to reveal Mt Discovery close up in lovely late-season lighting.

We approach 'resort Black Island': two distinctive 15m-tall geodesic golf balls housing satellite dish receivers and a cluster of buildings and fuel tanks, four windmills and three chimneys from Ormat furnaces.

Distant Ross Island, with Erebus and McMurdo, and Scott Base just visible, looks unusual from this angle.

Power for this installation is generated using both wind and Ormat oil furnaces. Smoke moves more vertically than horizontally and the windmills are just turning. Little wind. We're lucky, considering this site's reputation for 100+ knot winds, which really rattle the light kevlar skin on the domes.

Crossing the Ross Ice Shelf to Black Island

Top: Black Island's two 15m-tall geodesic golf-balls at sunrise. Below: 'Dirty' ice from Black Island.

GREG WILKINSON: KIWI JANITOR IN 'MACTOWN'

'Your shit is our bread and butter!' So went the unofficial motto for our janitorial crew of young(ish) Kiwis at Mactown (McMurdo) in the early 1990s. And with McMurdo being very much a reflection of the throwaway American society, we cleaners were certainly never short of a sandwich or two.

While not the most glamorous job in the McMurdo social strata, the opportunity to housekeep for the Americans was a rare chance for this itinerant Kiwi to indulge in the ultimate overseas experience – an Antarctic winter-over. As the boss told me once, 'It's not just a job, it's a lifestyle.'

And what a unique and thrilling lifestyle it was. I was part of a minority group of up to 100 New Zealanders – from cleaners, defence force cargo handlers and administration staff to field assistants and even the occasional scientist – working as the 'logistical support personnel' at McMurdo for the summer season. In the winter of 1993 we numbered just 13 in a McMurdo population of 237.

As far as Antarctic research stations go, McMurdo is a metropolis, catering to the needs of 1000-plus citizens over the summer. All the creature comforts of home, and recreational and entertainment activities galore add up to a very desirable escapist lifestyle. The bright sodium-vapour lights illuminate the winter night like the neon signs in Las Vegas.

Though outnumbered by the Americans we Kiwis proudly contributed more than our share of cultural input to the unique American-Kiwi community that exists on Ross Island. We learned about Halloween, Thanksgiving, Independence Day, chilli cook-off competitions, gridiron, Garth Brooks and Budweiser (aka 'butt-wiper'), and added a New Zealand flavour that was usually well received by our hosts.

From amidst the hoopla of Americana at McMurdo, Scott Base stood out like a beacon, providing a direct link with home and a very welcome change of cultural environment, especially over the winter months: a phone and fax service, a shop that sold Vegemite and chocolate fish and accepted New Zealand currency, the slang, the humour and the kinship while sharing a familiar brew at the bar.

On a political level McMurdo and Scott Base may

Greg Wilkinson and Viv Taylor

have observed formal protocols but among the great unwashed there existed a congenial neighbourliness and curiosity. There were many social encounters through sport, 'open nights' at the bar and theme parties where friendships were forged and the occasional romance blossomed. At one such party I compared janitorial methods with Scott Base winter GD (domestic) Vivienne Taylor and we now share the cleaning roster at our home in Cromwell.

Scott Basers tended to enjoy greater freedom of travel around Ross Island than most at McMurdo. Because of the size of population McMurdo-ites were restricted to within a few kilometres of base unless you could score yourself a 'boondoggle' (fam). I admit to being envious of the Scott Base 'fam trips' to Cape Evans and Cape Royds and frustrated at not being allowed to join them.

Sadly the humble Kiwi janitor is now an extinct species at McMurdo, the contract having been taken over by ASA in 1994. My certificate for the Antarctica Service Medal awarded by NSFA says 'in recognition of valuable contributions to explorations to scientific achievement under the US Antarctic Program [sic]'. I am proud to have been part of this otherwise unsung New Zealand chapter in Antarctic history.

[Greg Wilkinson, also known as 'Jed McJed', worked for New Zealand contractor Fisher Catering during the summer of 1991-92, then Quality Service Enterprises during the summer/winter of 1992-93.]

Mitch Perry has the jug on as we pull up, and later insists that we partake of his ricotta and tomato pasta dish. Jeff and an elf-like Al Oxton (with purple tights, colourful jersey, jester's hat and long grey beard tied in a knot) remain logged in on their computers. These self-confessed computer geeks dine on e-mail as well as food. Eventually they warm to our presence.

Dave and I sleep out in a tent; the temperature goes down to -36°C. The next day our return home is delayed eight hours by electrical problems with H-26, which keep Dave and John busy on the phone to Joe. We drive home in the dark without any possums or rabbits streaking ahead in our headlights. I manage to shoot three rolls of 36-exposure film while I'm away.

The next day is Thursday, open night. We've counted and we celebrate our half a year on ice with a halfway party – half-price drinks, half-hourly for half the night.

Al, Jeff and Mitch from Black Island are definites on the guest list of 30 for our celebratory sunset dinner on 25 April. We won't see the sun for another four months!

That day is not only Anzac Day, but also Festa della Liberazione (Italy's Liberation Day). Our flag is lowered to half mast when twilight shows near

Antarctic rabbits caught in the headlights

morning tea time. Scotty serves some Anzac biscuits and, with Jan, continues preparing the evening's Italian feast.

Going Italian allows Scotty to prepare a superb meal without too much need for fresh produce – it's been two months since the last plane departed. With limited resources we'll allow Scotty to substitute, just a little.

Antipasto, focaccia and various pastas and pizzas abound. Tomato, snapper, prawns, anchovies, chicken, salami, olives, capers, garlic, fetta, parmesan, mozzarella and cream, in various combinations, form generous toppings and sauces. A centrepiece five-litre bottle of chianti makes one round of 40 glasses before other wines are opened.

Scotty's handcrafted cioccolata (chocolate) cups with gelato balls are the evening's *pièce de resistance*. Three ices, appropriately coloured, are served: red

Festa della Liberazione dinner: Scotty with Bob Rehmel, Joe and Gail Noton, left, and Gary Teestell, Karen Schwall and Scott Humpert, right.

(boysenberry cassata), white (cashew, coconut and Cointreau – okay, a little French) and green (Galliano and Midori), all served with crescent-shaped aniseed chrabeli. Our guests now know we have the best chef on Ross Island this winter.

Speeches, coffee and biscotti, with an Amaretto, Galliano or Sambuca, complete the evening.

The plaudits follow, with Al Oxton suggesting that New Zealand Post print a Ross Dependency postage stamp to commemorate the occasion – a macaroni penguin on a pizza iceberg.

Word gets around McMurdo and some of those not invited feel snubbed. Such is a dilemma of living in a small closed society.

Satellite communication is big at McMurdo. Jeff Smith reports to a town meeting that an average of 7000 e-mail transactions are made each day. That's equivalent to each person generating or receiving about 28 transactions! Much of this mail is official, to offices in the United States in Washington DC (NSF), Denver (ASA) or Port Humeme (NSFA).

E-mail users can become impatient if replies aren't prompt. Communicating between different time zones adds to the frustration. ASA's Denver office in the central United States is 19 hours behind McMurdo.

At one town meeting a solution is suggested. As we're insulated from the outside world, we should adopt central United States time. Of course Scott Base would have to go along with this too for the system to work. Another suggestion is for an international date line at the top of the hill between Scott Base and McMurdo and three zones in McMurdo, equating to western (Port Humeme), central (Denver) and eastern (Washington DC) time. Both ideas are dismissed.

Because McMurdo staff need to venture outside in all weathers to get to the galley and because food prepared for 244 often isn't as good as food for one, many citizens cook for themselves. Their self-contained rooms contain limited cooking facilities and the store sells foodstuffs for personal use. Also, zip-lock plastic bags are provided at the servery for takeaways.

Of course this means personal interaction suffers as a consequence. Sometimes it seems it's easier to continue relationships with family and friends in another part of the world via e-mail than to break the ice with the stranger in the room down the hallway.

Those in McMurdo without access to work computers still need to visit the galley. Their electronic narcotic 'fix' is available on the public-use computers set up there during winter.

At open meeting town manager Al claims the town is going into hibernation, with only 20 turning out for breakfast.

Women might not be the only reason McMurdo is losing its frontier-town image. Maybe the computer screen is just as influential.

11

15 JUNE '95 - AIRDROP DAY

It's almost 0730 – a significant daily moment in the continuum of winter. Time to rise. Showered and dressed, I head down to the mess, take a glass of chilled lemon cordial, then some tinned fruit and cornflakes doused with reconstituted milk. At the table John, Joe and Scotty are already eating, while Dave cooks bacon and eggs out in the kitchen.

Dave likes his cooked breakfast – some of his winter works programme projects are rather physical. I spend most of my winter at a desk and, with my weight climbing, I again resist the daily torture – the wafting smell of bacon! Eggs last 10 months down here. Before leaving New Zealand they are coated in oil, which forms a preservative barrier.

The same old faces at the table generally arrive in the same order, day in, day out, with John first and Jim last.

Breakfast on 15 June prompts thoughts of today's event. There should be freshly sliced fruit on this plate tomorrow. NSFA officer in charge, Scott Humpert, called me on my bedroom telephone before 0700 and confirmed that the C-141 Starlifter had departed Christchurch with an ETA of 1130. Today we receive our midwinter airdrop.

Airdrop approaches with burning oil drums marking the drop zone on the Ross Ice Shelf
and Scott Base in the foreground

It's not surprising to learn that Scott's message has already circulated – has Scotty learned of it before returning from McMurdo?

He spends many nights over there now. Last month our chef attended the McMurdo housing co-ordinator's birthday and won her over with his 'death by chocolate' cups, printed with a flag and the words 'Happy Birthday Hope'. Romance is in the air and the grin on his face has been saying it all, as does Hope Stout's.

Before the airdrop arrives, other tasks need attention. I check the administration mailbox for any incoming e-mail that may require forwarding but, unlike McMurdo, we're lucky to receive any.

At 0815 on Thursday mornings John and I speak to Gill and Malcolm in Christchurch via our weekly teleconference and, as expected, today's airdrop dominates this morning's conversation. Further mention is made of the decision declining my one-off request to allow seven of the team to leave base to be at this year's drop. Three left on base for a couple of hours is considered too risky if things go wrong, so a fire crew of five must remain. In past years there have been two airdrops so everyone has had a chance to be involved.

While outside taking the 0900 met observations I notice that a light 8/8 cover of high-stratus cloud is diffusing the near full-moon light, yet there's still enough reflection from our snowy surroundings to see beyond 50km. This weather won't prevent the airdrop.

Yesterday was marginal so Scott erred on the side of caution and postponed the drop. Three days ago the airdrop mission to Amundsen-Scott South Pole Station had to be called off because it was too wet in Christchurch. They wouldn't fly the KC-10 tanker aeroplane, which refuels the Starlifter on its flight south, as they could have had problems relanding this fuel-laden plane if the mission had had to be aborted. The weather at the Pole was perfect that day.

Back inside Scotty is paging me for an incoming call. Scott Humpert has news. The plane is flying with a tail wind and now has an ETA of 1030.

Bruce, Jim, John and Tom have volunteered to remain at home, so only Scotty is disappointed to be missing out on the action. The rest dress quickly, grab cameras and drive in H-26 out to the ice shelf Williams Field runway, where two rows of burning oil drums mark the drop zone. Ahead of us the procession of headlights indicates that McMurdo has mobilised.

For many of McMurdo's Operations Team this shared drop is the highlight of their winter, with many hours of preparation and planning. Many of ASA Gerald (Rocky) Ness's team are regular winter-over returnees and many have done this before. Big Sam Williams, the heavy equipment foreman, has hardly seen better. He reckons -18°C without wind is almost tropical.

Sam's boys have a large fleet of vehicles assembled; each huge wheeled or tracked vehicle has an assigned task. Once our booty is dropped, the first to the scene will have tall multi-direction lighting towers that will illuminate the surroundings like a sportsground. Others will follow: flat-decks, warm storage units, forklifts and cranes. Teams have the task of quickly mopping up, should any packages break open. The fire/crash crew and a JASART team

A delayed-exposure shot of the approaching C-141

Scott Base's freshies package on its side (left); McMurdo baker Trine Gjorstad and team quickly rescue theirs

wait in pre-determined formation at the front of the staging apron. There's a continual buzz of radio transmission between vehicles and the control tower.

Many people from McMurdo have assembled. The balmy conditions draw people out from vehicles and high spirits are evident – it's like waiting for Santa. The serious photographic brigade set up tripods and keep their cameras warm inside their jackets.

To the north-west a singular light appears like a distant satellite, still some 10 minutes or so out. The control tower orders all vehicle lights off and radio communication to cease, to assist the flight crew on approach. Revelry ceases and all eyes fix on the distant aircraft. It's time for time-delay photographs.

The single light divides into two then, a little later, more, with the C-141 becoming better defined on its low-angle approach, lining up on the two rows of flaming oil drums. Closer, closer, lights transform to include the sound of the engines. We're almost within touching distance.

Hydraulic rams have already pushed the rear cargo door open and, with power applied, the craft climbs, disgorging a trail of 40 packages from less than 300ft above the deck. Some 25,500lb of load including 14,300lb of mail (the Americans still use pounds and feet) is ejected in seconds.

Spontaneous cheering muffles the popping as small parachutes open. From the safe confines of

the staging zone and under this milky moonlight we can make out the packages as they thud into the snow.

The well-rehearsed procedure is now put into action. Official clearance is given from the control tower and the vehicles idling stationary on the staging apron begin to roll.

Priority is given to packages identified by flashing strobe lights – those containing precious DNF (do not freeze) freshies. They're loaded into warm storage units.

Excitedly, we look for Scott Base's three, which are discernible by their yellow kiwi labels. There's dismay when it's discovered that ours with the strobe has implanted itself heavily on its side after its parachute failed to open. The small parachute is only intended to keep each package upright so that the half-metre of oversized corrugated cardboard on the base absorbs the impact. Our others appear to be in perfect condition.

Sam calls over the crane to extract our freshies package.

A McMurdo freshies package has broken open. A mop-up team makes light work of reducing freezing damage to the freshies as bagfuls are loaded into the warmth of a vehicle.

Another important issue has surfaced. ASA surveyors John Sale and Tom Moody have run a sweepstake in which $US10 bought one of 200 surveyed

PETER MCKAY: ORION NZ4201'S WINTER FLIGHT

The two flight engineers, F/Lt Sid Elliott and F/Sgt Vern Reynolds, conducted a detailed inspection of the aircraft in seven degrees of frost. Inside the aircraft the three radio/radar operators, Sqn Ldr Jack Hewson, Master AEOp 'Junior' Senior and F/Sgt 'Baldy' Auld, carefully checked their systems. F/Sgt Gus Parcell prepared an excellent breakfast in the aircraft's galley and made a final check of our precious cargo.

In the warmth of the terminal building the two navigators, Sqn Ldr Stewart Quayle and F/Off Terry Gardiner, completed the detailed navigation flight plan. About them hovered the aircraft's captain, Wing Commander Peter McKay, who anxiously watched the navigator's computations. F/Off Alex Stevens, the co-pilot, consulted the aircraft's operating manual and extracted all the data applicable to the take-off from Dunedin.

The weather forecast indicated strong winds so we were in for a long flight – calculated to be 12 hours 27 minutes. Before daybreak at 0654 on 1 August 1973 Orion 4201 climbed to 28,000ft and headed south.

The United States Navy had approached RNZAF Air Staff to investigate the possibility of a winter mail delivery. Detailed studies by the No. 5 (Orion) Squadron concluded that with a departure from Dunedin the Orion could safely make the 4500-mile (7200km) round trip without a landing. The plane's excellent three-engine range performance, should an engine be lost over McMurdo, would get it home. A comforting thought.

Due to the unreliability of the magnetic compass in high latitudes, a training flight well south of New Zealand was made early in July to test grid navigation techniques and the inertial navigation system.

With Antarctic survival equipment supplied by Operation Deep Freeze, and the need to carry the maximum 30 tons of fuel, only 840lb of mail (50lb of it for Scott Base) packaged in special containers could be carried.

The flight south was uneventful but impressive. The sun scarcely rose above the horizon and it progressively became more gloomy the further south

Peter McKay

we flew. There was sufficient light over the continent to see vast expanses of ice, mountains and glaciers. In this light, an eerie sight.

Descent over McMurdo was made at 1227 and, 10 minutes later, the aircraft dropped below the overcast conditions with landing lights on. Dead ahead was the drop zone. The lights of McMurdo and the drop zone were quite bright, yet visual contact with the ground would have been possible without them in the murky twilight.

On the first run two of the six containers were dispatched. Their parachutes failed to deploy properly but soft snow saved them. On the second run a hitch with cabin pressurisation prevented the door from opening. On the third, one of the two containers broke open, raining mail on the people below. We were happy to learn later that only some newspapers and magazines were lost. The final run was perfect.

We soared to 29,000ft and headed for Dunedin, ETA 1925. As we flew north in increasing daylight, a calm settled over the crew. Only one navigation 'let down' aid was usable over McMurdo and this had played on our minds, especially with Mt Erebus nearby. We could now relax and enjoy the awesome spectacle of hundreds of miles of Antarctic landscape – the pack ice disappearing behind us about halfway home.

The flight was quite an experience. Temperatures down to -53°C were measured outside the aircraft.

Throughout the flight the radio operators were extremely busy and on the homeward leg the messages of sincere appreciation from McMurdo buoyed our spirits.

Orion 4201 touched down at Dunedin at 1920 – 12 hours and 26 minutes after departing. Our calculations were only one minute out!

[Wing Commander Peter McKay has now retired from the RNZAF and lives in Whangarei.]

One of Sam Williams's machines picking up a package

segments of the designated drop zone. If a particular numbered package from the drop fell in your segment, the $US1000 first prize would be yours. There were minor prizes up for grabs too. The problem is, the drop has fallen off to the side of the drop zone.

The eventual winners are drawn at random at McMurdo's airdrop party the following weekend.

Sam's team makes light work of the operation and the site is quickly cleared. We join the procession of headlights leading back to base.

Tom is waiting with the loader to off-load our two non-DNF packages from a flat-deck. For Tom, handling cargo makes a welcome change from months of preparing field equipment. Our packages are deposited into the cold porch of the garage and are enthusiastically opened.

Our mail is sorted in the bar. For the rest of the afternoon we're ensconced, emotions mixed, among

piles of letters and packages – a whole host of the practical, the impractical and consumable. Generosity of vulgar proportion has been showered on us by families and friends at home and it makes even Christmas look a little sad. People's interpretations of the material needs missing from our lives down here are quite varied and original.

Personal yield varies, but it has never been disputed, during the time leading up to airdrop, who's likely to get the most. In a secret campaign to knock Scotty off his perch I outpoint him with the number of letters, but fall well short on parcel volume.

During the afternoon our neighbours deliver the mangled inner cartons from our freshies package. Tell-tale dampness confirms Scotty's worst fears: 'half tossed salad and half fruit juice'. We're looking at salvaging maybe 10 per cent. Preparing exciting dishes without freshies is a challenge, especially

Bruce surveys the damage, but Scotty's attentions are otherwise engaged

for a chef with such flamboyance. But the excitement of the moment, with most still busily reading personal mail, offsets any disappointment.

Fresh food in the middle of winter isn't really necessary for survival or good nutrition – it's more of a treat and is good for morale. The deficiency diseases early explorers suffered, such as scurvy, are pretty much impossible today. Our plentiful supply of frozen food (meat, vegetables and some fruit) along with baked bread and cereals, forms the basis of our nutrionally balanced diet. There is less reliance these days on dehydrated or tinned food. A 'hobby scale' hydroponics unit provides a little greenery and there are plenty of sprouts.

After dinner Sean drives up to Arrival Heights to undertake the monthly Dobson spectrometer measurements. Using the full moon's light, the intensity can be correlated to ozone levels. The cloud has peeled back, giving a good image of the moon for Sean to focus on tonight. Last night too much cloud allowed him to focus on three or four cans of Guinness for his birthday instead.

With not much happening, Scotty and Joe take one of the Toyotas and head over to McMurdo for the night. Three Toyotas are kept up and running during winter and we always endeavour to keep one at base at all times. Sean isn't far away on his return from the Heights so I sign out, take the third vehicle and drive across to McMurdo's aerobics gym.

Thursday is one of my regular exercise evenings and I burn off 1100 calories on a Lifestepper machine. No one else is in the gym tonight so I crank up Little Feat's 'Time Loves a Hero' on the stereo. I sip away on my new sports drink bottle containing electrolyte drink; Liz sent the bottle and a couple of cans of Restore powder in the airdrop.

Driving home, I notice through the gap between Observation and Crater hills that most of the oil drums out at Williams Field have gone out. I reflect on the almost certainty that this year's airdrop has signalled the end of the luxury Ross Island's winter society has enjoyed since 1973, to be cut for economic reasons.

12

THE HIGHS

Much of the magic of winter is the spectacle of its beginning, happening then finishing. Summer staff may savour a méthode champenoise Antarctic experience, but it's those privileged to winter over who enjoy the champagne.

During winter Antarctica really performs. The continent's natural phenomena are accentuated: the wind is windier, the cold colder and the dryness drier (if the increased level of static electricity discharge is any measure). The greatest impact going into and coming out of winter is visual.

Spectacular light brings to life the comparatively austere flat whites and blues of the summer landscape. Each day the view of the expansive ice shelf, sea ice and distant peaks is revitalised as within two months the sun goes from being above the horizon the whole day to being below it all day. The sun rises at a particular spot on the eastern horizon during breakfast one morning, then the next, it rises noticeably further northward and noticeably later.

The reds and golds become redder and golder; then there's the black.

Another sort of Black Magic is the subject of much pleasure during our month of May.

Most of our neighbours hail from the central United States, miles away from any ocean. This conveniently becomes the basis of denial of any interest in yachting, but there is always a twinkle in their eyes when they say, 'Who the hell is Dennis Conner anyway?'

By Tuesday, Team New Zealand in San Diego has sailed to a 2-0 margin so it's agreed that this Saturday night's Scott Base monthly party will be a diesel and drummi party. With any luck, the Kiwis will by then be wrapping up the regatta uncontested. Team New Zealand is faxed best wishes for the coming weekend from the most remote team of Kiwis on the planet.

We've plenty of diesel (Steinlager) on offer. Each slab is raided for application forms so our guests can join Team New Zealand's Supporters' Club, albeit retrospectively.

A drummi is an environmentally friendly mechanical hangi – a 44-gallon drum with nesting baskets and an extended base to accommodate gas burners. In effect, it's an oversized steamer.

Each summer Kiwi defence force cargo handlers living at McMurdo have traditionally put down a hangi for the Americans. But this summer overzealous interpretation of the Madrid Protocol ruled out an umu in McMurdo's scoria, so John, our amenable

Jan and Scotty attend to our drummi

97

engineer, and master cargo handler and hangi guru Wayne Henry came to the rescue and constructed a drummi. These are used in other parts of the world on New Zealand defence force assignments.

Scotty puts his artistic skills to good use and embellishes a black-painted drummi with a silver fern, and words 'Team New Zealand' and 'Black Magic'.

Saturday arrives with New Zealand 4-0 up. The drummi delivers again, feeding an extra 40 for dinner, and another 40 come to hear the second public performance for this winter of McMurdo's band, Bandayboo.

Bandayboo's repertoire is an interesting blend. Rex Cortner is distinctly country and western on acoustic guitar and vocals, while younger guitarist and drummer Mark Lopus and Scott Enlow prefer a heavier rock/alternative style. Slop slaps out some bass. Improvisation is important in Antarctica and their live interactive music is thoroughly enjoyed by those who dance the night away oblivious to the 4-0 margin.

Peter Montgomery's commentary on Radio New Zealand International's shortwave is exceptionally clear the following morning. Dennis is blown off the water 5-0.

NZAP receptionist Donna Walls's daily e-mail summary of Monday's news includes mention of Jim Bolger's suggestion that employers give staff a day off to celebrate. We justify one for ourselves – after all, we have not spent the last week or so around an office television set.

It might be a day off but I can't miss McMurdo's town meeting and the opportunity to play Queen's 'We are the Champions' at almost subliminal volume on a Walkman with mini-speakers hidden in my pockets. There are further denials of any interest in yachting.

Our winter solstice falls at exactly 0800 on 22 June 1995. The Beatles' 'Here Comes the Sun' plays while the team heads off to work after breakfast, and while Jim starts eating his. The sun begins moving south.

We exchange faxed messages of goodwill with winter-over teams at the two other American bases, Amundsen-Scott South Pole and Palmer; four Australian bases, Casey, Davis, Mawson and Macquarie; five British bases, Faraday, Halley, Rothera, Signy and Bird Island; French base Dumont d'Urville; German base Neumayer; and Chinese base the Great Wall Station.

It's unfortunate no team is wintering over at South Africa's SANAE base this winter, so no fax is sent there. In hindsight this is maybe just as well, for the

An acoustic concert: Sandy Grandchamp, Bobby Lozano and Marcello DelGiudice performing

Dave Navas, Sean and John at a hat party

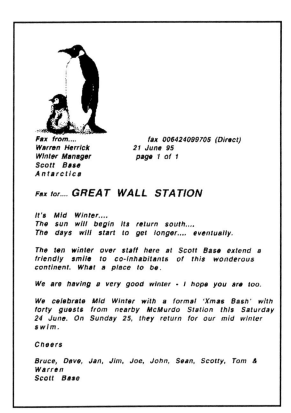

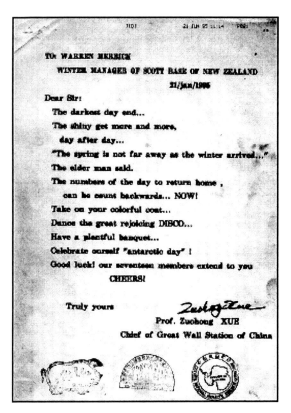

All Blacks are challenging strongly for the Rugby World Cup in South Africa and Donna's e-mail news is full of Jonah Lomu's exploits.

Coincidentally our planned formal midwinter Christmas dinner falls on the eve of the World Cup final. This time 40 guests are invited. Scotty works hard to concoct a feast from the remnants of our airdrop, together with some goodies coerced from our friendly neighbours.

David (Woody) Porter of the Crary Laboratory wrote an e-mail account of the occasion:

Who were these people attending this function? Gone were the dowdy, dull, worn-out clothes seen in previous months. Instead there were purple sequins, sheer black fabrics, beautiful turquoise velvet, bright colours, suit coats, vests and ties. Hair was styled – even brushed or combed. Showers had been taken before dining, make-up was evident and that faint smell? Could it be perfume?

This olfactory stimulation is augmented by Scotty's fare of cranberry-stuffed roast turkey, venison, pork and local cod poached in Sambuca. The vegetable selection is a little more unorthodox with julienne carrot and leek, battered turnip fingers, sauteed curried cabbage along with his château potatoes. Parsley garnishes most dishes. Christmas pud with brandy sauce, pavlova, chocolate profiteroles, 'real' Kiwi icecream and cheeses complete the feast.

The night continues until well after the late news and weather back home in New Zealand, but our guests return home by shuttle bus before the 0100 kick-off. They obviously can't face any further gloating. We're convinced Jonah will have scored at least three tries before half-time.

Rugby live on the radio in the wee hours of the morning – it takes me back. Radio reception begins fading in and out. By 0300 it's hard to hear exactly what is going on but it seems we've lost so, finishing the last of the port, we head for bed.

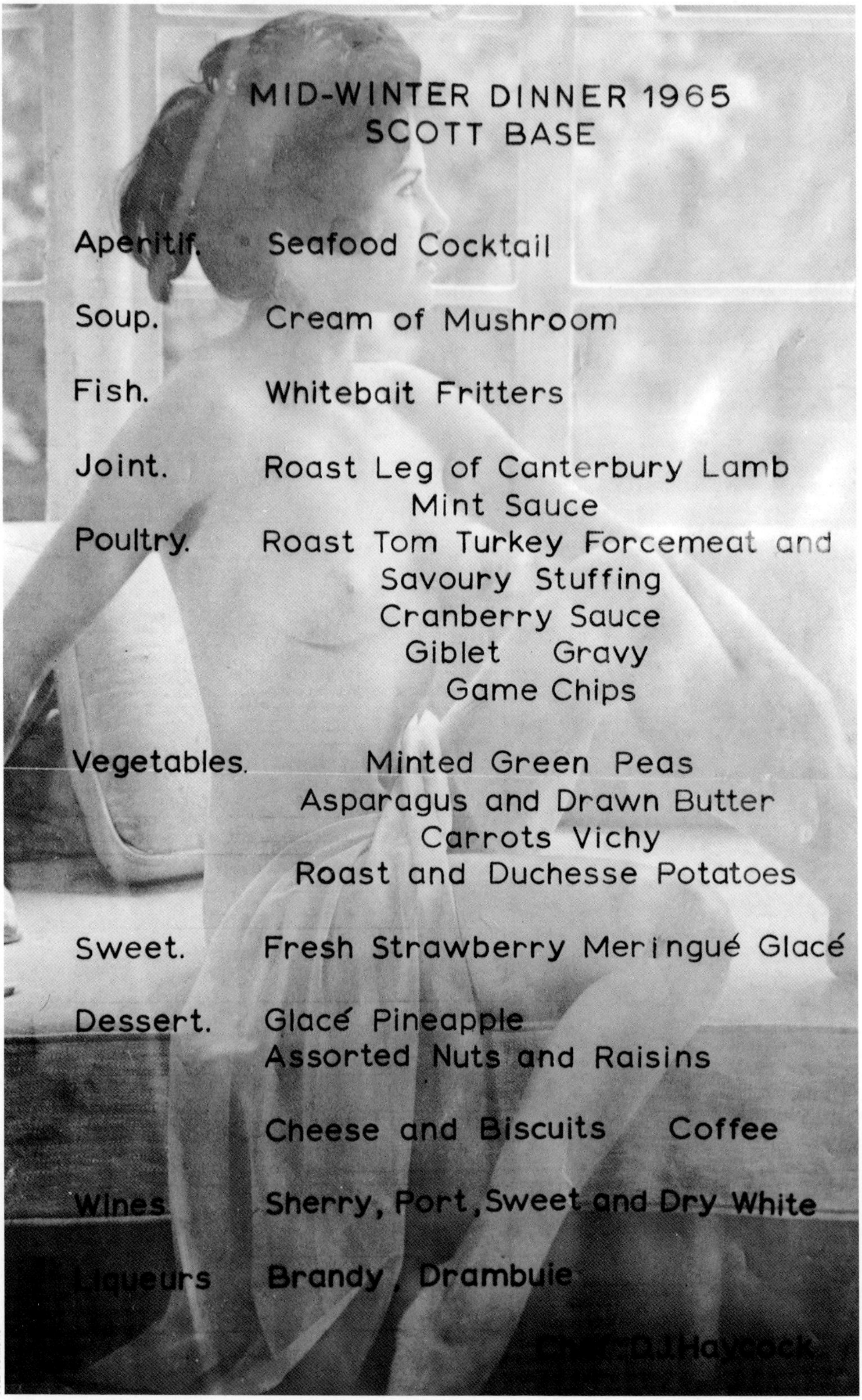

MID-WINTER DINNER 1965
SCOTT BASE

Aperitif. Seafood Cocktail

Soup. Cream of Mushroom

Fish. Whitebait Fritters

Joint. Roast Leg of Canterbury Lamb
Mint Sauce

Poultry. Roast Tom Turkey Forcemeat and
Savoury Stuffing
Cranberry Sauce
Giblet   Gravy
Game Chips

Vegetables. Minted Green Peas
Asparagus and Drawn Butter
Carrots Vichy
Roast and Duchesse Potatoes

Sweet. Fresh Strawberry Meringué Glacé

Dessert. Glacé Pineapple
Assorted Nuts and Raisins

Cheese and Biscuits   Coffee

Wines Sherry, Port, Sweet and Dry White

Liqueurs Brandy , Drambuie

Chef D.J.Haycock.

BUZZ BURROWS

A creative mind has always been present at Scott Base: the midwinter Christmas menu 1965

Americans have dominated world swimming for years and accordingly it's not surprising many are eager to take part in our midwinter polar plunge. McMurdo's regulations don't permit them to conduct swims of their own but a blind eye is turned to those wishing to take part in ours.

Our crew is interested in only one swim this winter, and then mainly only to appease those at McMurdo. Most winter-over teams cut open the hole in the sea ice for sunset, midwinter and sunrise swims and our break in tradition tests the patience of some of our neighbours. One regular swimmer in past years, Maddison Hall, strongly objects to our relaxed stance allowing the wearing of swimsuits and boycotts the event.

McMurdo's patience is further tested. Constant 25-30 knot winds, gusting to 40, temperatures around -23°C push the windchill below -50°C. We consider it's unsafe and delay the event.

Tom, with John lending some assistance, put in 32 hours of effort, first cutting through more than two metres of old ice (which didn't break out during summer), then maintaining the hole as it continually refreezes.

Over 60 enthusiasts swim the next weekend, some doing it twice. With 0-5 knot winds at -30°C the windchill is less than -33°C.

Outswum in terms of enthusiasm for the polar plunge, Scott Base's Nocturnal Birds (Kiwis) are also well and truly out-bowled during the winter's 10-pin bowling competition. We are relegated to the lower league after the first round and finish last in the second round.

We enjoy bowling without the pressure of having to win games. Personal-best scores become more important, as well as avoiding earning a 'chicken' (bowling three gutter balls in a row). Occasionally Bruce, our team's kingpin, throws down a 'turkey' (three 10-pin strikes in a row) and he often scores reasonably highly. Dave, Jim and Sean regularly achieve scores of three figures, while Jan, John, Scotty and I mostly register twos.

Early in March, however, there is an aberration that deserves to be recorded for posterity. Nocturnal Birds score *no* chickens and blast away one of the better teams on the lanes with a 523-490 win over the Firehouse. Our team card: Bruce 185, Dave 140, Scotty 92 and Warren 106 – all personal-best scores. We win only one other game for the season.

Another aberration is Scotty's 208, with the first five balls sent down being strikes. Unfortunately the points don't count as it's only a practice night.

Scotty's interest falls off when he is unable to match the 208 and he begins to direct his energies to darts. On Friday nights it's International Darts on Ice against, in Scotty words, 'the rest of the world'. At 2100 (our time) Australian bases Casey and Davis and Amundsen-Scott at the South Pole regularly come up on 5400HF radio. Despite occasional ionospheric disturbance, relay assistance usually gets most scores though.

Scotty's enthusiasm focuses not only on darts but on performing to a radio audience and teasing the Aussies. Along with Terry Trimingham, Ed Stockard and Hope from McMurdo, Bruce and Sean regularly make up Scott Base's team.

Scotty trying for another 208!

MAX QUINN: CAPE CROZIER REVISITED

As Cherry-Garrard recounts in his book *The Worst Journey in the World*: 'The horror of the nineteen days it took us to travel from Cape Evans to Cape Crozier would have to be re-experienced to be appreciated ... and anyone would be a fool who went again ... '

Eighty years later and with these words firmly implanted in our minds Don and I set out rather apprehensively to retrace the footsteps of Wilson, Bowers and Cherry-Garrard in 1911. We were working on a television documentary on the emperor penguin.

Max Quinn (right) and Don Anderson

No fools, we travelled the easy way – in the warmth of a Hagglunds. An eight-hour journey across the Ross Ice Shelf followed a flagged route to our huts, navigating with way-points logged in on our GPS. Even so, some dark winter journeys had their moments, enough to reinforce our highest respect for those explorers. Whiteouts, difficulty spotlighting reflectors on the next flag and the risk of wandering too far off the route increased the danger of straying into a crevasse.

Our periodic trips to Cape Crozier – we did 13 in all – were timed to coincide with the various stages of the unique breeding cycle of the emperor.

Late summer filming followed the birds on the sea ice, fattening themselves in readiness for their long winter vigil. With the onset of autumn, and temperatures rapidly plunging below -30°C, the sea's freezing is surely one of the natural world's most spectacular sights. The heat variation between air and water causes the sea to 'smoke'.

We were at Crozier in April to coincide with the penguins' arrival at the breeding site. Unable to film on the sea ice as it was still too weak, I filmed from the shore in a raging herbie. The penguins emerged from the blowing snow like ghosts. They seemed to sympathise with our predicament, coming surprisingly close as they tobogganed in long lines, allowing me to capture some of the most evocative footage of our winter journeys.

We returned with the returning sun in August. This was a glorious time to be filming. The chicks were hatching and the parents were returning to and from the open sea with fish dinners for their young.

We normally shoot natural history on 16mm film but opted for videotape here, as we had no chance of getting the film back to New Zealand for processing. Don's do-it-yourself skills turned out a specially-made jacket incorporating heating powered by a 12-volt battery, which kept the camera working in the cold. The camera's battery power would be sapped within an hour or so, but by then we would be glad to be heading back up the slope to the relative warmth of our hut. We could relish a welcome whiskey with, of course, ice chipped from the hut's inside wall.

In July 1911 Scott wrote in his diary after the return of the heroic trio: '... that man should wander forth into the depths of a polar night to face the most dismal cold and fiercest gale ... makes a tale for our generation which I hope may not be lost in the telling.'

It was truly our hope that the films we made during the winter of 1991 upheld those glorious sentiments. And for as long as I live I will not forget the sight of these incredible birds huddling together in the dark.

[Max Quinn and Don Anderson wintered over in 1990-91 and produced two TVNZ Natural History Unit films that are available on video: *Emperors of Antarctica* and *The Longest Winter*, the latter following the activities of the winter-over team.]

The game they play is 501 – a double to start, wipe off all the points, then finish with the double required to finish on zero. Playing order depends on previous results, with the leading team playing last, and each player throws three darts in turn. The results from each base are broadcast to the rest. A high degree of honesty is obviously required.

Scott Base finishes third – an honourable result considering the slight element of doubt regarding the scores from the perimeter of the continent.

The wind blows stronger on the continent's perimeter, where the Aussie bases are located. Reports of 50-60 knot winds at Scott Base during darts nights are received by the Aussies with much mirth. Their countryman Mawson set up his base in 1911 at Commonwealth Bay, the windiest place on earth, where winds blow up to three times as strong.

This winter we occasionally communicate with an Australian couple wintering over at Commonwealth Bay. Don and Margie McIntyre are on a private expedition and living in a 2.4m x 3.6m hut and endure temperatures down to -19°C inside the hut, condensation problems and monotony. Their regular communications (their trip was sponsored by Telecom) with schools in Australia, New Zealand, the United States and Japan help keep their spirits up.

When wind blows consistently stronger than 55 knots and visibility drops below 30m, 'Condition One' is called. There is a sense of excitement when such weather ceases all vehicular traffic and restricts foot travel to the immediate vicinity of base, and only for good reason.

Most herbies at Scott Base are associated with cyclonic weather systems, with centres passing several hundred kilometres east or north-east. Squally

Snow drifting in the evening light of summer

southerly winds blow in blizzard proportions and, particularly during winter, temperatures rise when stagnant cold surface air is displaced by warmer air cycled in from the north. During August 1995, with its mean temperature of -28.3°C (the coldest part of the year), one herbie gusts up to 56 knots from the south and takes the mercury soaring to -7.8°C!

Both Bruce and Jim have an uncanny knack of being out when herbies kick in. Often Bruce is off cross-country skiing and Jim is either at or travelling to (or from) our satellite earth station.

When the anemometer dials start registering southerlies in the 40-50 knot region there are special trips up to the Hatherton Laboratory to read the continuous printout on the anemograph. Scott Base stands defiant to all wind and, from the security inside, everyone secretly wills the needle to wind off the anemometer dial.

The weather forecast is favourable. Only Dave, Scotty and I are keen to camp out in darkness at Turtle Rock on a fam trip. Bruce, Jim and Sean opt to make a day trip at a future date.

Under July's full moon, once the clouds have finally peeled away, we whisk along the iceshelf on two snow-mobiles, each pulling a laden sledge. From the skifield, we point uphill to Castle Rock, then pause for the view.

Away from the range of Scott Base's lighting

Bruce returns from cross-country skiing

tower our eyes adjust to the moonlight. In this friendly milky opalescent light Mt Erebus appears splendid as it issues a horizontal plume of smoke. It's obviously windier up there than down here, where it's basically calm and only about -25°C.

We travel north along Hut Point Peninsula's windswept sastrugi, which slow progress. The transition onto the sea ice is easily crossed, leaving a short run over smooth sea ice to Turtle Rock – a silhouetted mass of volcanic terra firma.

Once the ski-mobile engines are cut the tranquillity is blissful and feelings of isolation overwhelm. Only the distant glow in the sky to the south – McMurdo – reveals any other human presence. We pitch our tent.

Atop 50m Turtle Rock is a good place to drink the contents of a large thermos of hot chocolate laced with Stone's Green Ginger Wine and reflect.

Thoughts extend to Edward Wilson, 'Birdie' Bowers and Apsley Cherry-Garrard's 1911 winter trip to Cape Crozier to collect emperor penguin eggs – the trip dubbed the worst journey in the world. They passed nearby, further out on the sea ice, and recorded a temperature of -77°F (-61°C) on that trip – more than twice as cold as we are at the moment. With their lesser clothing and equipment they must have been tough. Bowers, in particular, had a reputation for withstanding cold.

When I get back to Scott Base I must reply to a fax recently received from Carl Blackmun from Christchurch – a young lad who has a burning desire to come here and who claims his great-great-uncle was Birdie Bowers.

With McMurdo's intensifying glow reflecting off building cloud it's time for bed. Never has a place seemed so appropriate for listening to some Pink Floyd – 'Meddle'. Snug in my bag, I plug into my Walkman for a while, then start drifting off with the tent door left open. What's that noise? Weddell seals beneath the ice!

Programmed to wake at 0720, we take a peek

Left: Dave with snow-mobiles in front of McMurdo Station. Right: Dave and Scotty at Turtle Rock camp.

out the tent door to see cloud enveloping us, but the Hutton Cliffs near our transition (where our flagged route home starts) are still visible. GPS won't be needed and with this cloud we can't return home on the sea ice.

Finding the flags at the transition proves a little harder than we expected and, sighting crevasses in our headlights, we backtrack. We find the flags again and scamper along the ridge's crest all the way to McMurdo, the intensifying winds stinging exposed flesh. From here we can take to the sea ice with rela-tive safety as long as we give Cape Armitage a wide berth. We pick up the distant beckoning glow of Scott Base's lighting tower before we lose McMurdo's lights and we easily make it home.

Scotty has been subdued on this trip as, moments before departing, he received news that his father is terminally ill with cancer. Scotty insisted we con-tinue with this trip, and has already asked if he can make a trip out to New Zealand to see his dad when Winfly starts in just over a month. The last months will be tough for him.

Ross Island with the lights of McMurdo and Scott Base, taken from Black Island

105

13

THE LOWS

The hardest part of winter is between airdrop and sunrise, we were told.

Parsley is the perfect freshie for airdrops, as a package of this virtually indestructible stuff wouldn't even need a parachute. Apart from a plentiful supply of carrot pieces and lettuce leaves, not much else has lasted. There's been no fresh fruit in the plate for breakfast.

The euphoria instilled by our airdrop mail and treats extends into the following week. But our thoughts soon turn to what may have been – crunching through an apple, tangy orange juice dribbling down the chin, some lightly salted tomato on toast. Our loss is now being felt.

The usual definition of a 'treat' doesn't apply here. Food mailed has been dominated by chocolate (chocolate blocks, chocolate bars, chocolate biscuits or just chocolates), and there are plenty of nuts too. But we have always had access to chocolate, at the base's shop. Here, with everything processed, refined, dried, preserved or frozen, sensory denial has induced a craving for the texture of the raw and fresh.

In addition to our freshies order crash-landing, it turns out it suffered another snag, the result of static electricity. This caused all three pages of the freshies order to stick together when being fed through the fax machine and, unbeknown to us, only one page was transmitted. The usual purchasing officer in Christchurch, Helen, was on annual leave and those filling in duly purchased and dispatched only the contents of the one-page list.

It seems that it did not occur to anyone in Christchurch that this was a very short list, missing many regular items. No one checked with us and we were none the wiser.

In light of the damage sustained, any bananas, kiwifruit and tomatoes wouldn't have survived anyway, but in our dark winter isolation we take the shortfall harder than we should.

We register our dismay and are particularly peeved at the reaction, a less-than-sympathetic: 'Your problem – you've only got another two months to Winfly.' A simple 'sorry about that, guys' would help.

In the grand plan of things it may seem that we're making a mountain out of a molehill, but from where we stand it is a big deal.

Scotty is aggrieved and Sean is particularly disappointed that his joke of ordering some party ice has also gone unappreciated. This is not a good way to be starting into the most difficult phase of winter. The insidiousness of winter's darkness is taking hold.

Having lived in a shadow for two months now, with virtually all-day darkness for the past four weeks, our physiology is modifying and our circadian rhythm is affected. This polar night increases the body's levels of melatonin, the chemical that maintains our biological clocks. A degree of depression is gradually induced, with an accompanying alteration of mood and function: classic 'winter blues', 'cabin fever' or 'seasonal affective disorder'. Our levels of the 'happy chemical' neurotransmitter serotonin are diminishing. Maybe John should dose our second-pass reverse osmosis water (our drinking water) with some Prozac.

Much has been written about the effects of winter's darkness and accounts by early polar explorers in both the Arctic and Antarctica give vivid descriptions of debilitation. Obviously their lack of physical comfort, emotional support and communication with the outside world contributed.

Modern bases with all their creature comforts (excluding freshies) and communication reduce the burden. Is it that we're getting softer?

Telecom is certainly doing its bit because for the month of June it is allowing Scott Base to be included in the $5 weekend deal. The usual phone cost to New Zealand of $1.48 + GST per minute usually restricts calls but with a maximum of $5 per call we now relax while chatting for two hours or more.

But this goes only so far in bridging the gap. We all have varying needs but none more than John, with two children back home.

Conflict is bound to surface in this unnatural environment. Monotony, close group interdependence and absence of the usual emotional gratification contribute to this stressed situation. With 10 people there are only 45 possible person-to-person interactions.

By all accounts, when compared with previous winter groups our team seems to be holding together well. After eight months everyone is fully aware of each other's traits. We are not always fully in agreement, but where conflict is likely to arise, common-sense usually prevails and inflammatory scenarios are avoided.

McMurdo is a handy diversion, especially for Joe, Scotty and Tom. When not on fire crew, Jim spends much of Sunday there with friends after church, and Dave heads to brunch at the galley most Sundays – he likes their orange juice and snow-freeze machine.

Everyone seems enthusiastic while going about their 0800-1700 business, an attitude important in averting boredom. Winter works programmes are well on their way to completion.

Scotty's food never fails to impress (apart from one memorable fish dish!). Jan's motivation with continual cleaning impresses and she enjoys a change in routine while preparing next season's first-aid kits. Preparing and maintaining for next season is Tom's constant lot – the tents have been repaired, he's filled the field food boxes and is now repairing sledges. Parts permitting, Sean's adaptability counters any technical challenge the Hatherton Lab or Arrival Heights throws his way. Jim keeps all communications links up, so what more can we ask of him?

John's engineering group continue to work as the team they have been since October. Their output is very impressive on their winter works programme, with at least another 50 per cent being attained, materials permitting. They are involved in

Winter works: Tom repairing lashings on a Tamworth sledge, left, and Dave maintains a cold-drinks machine

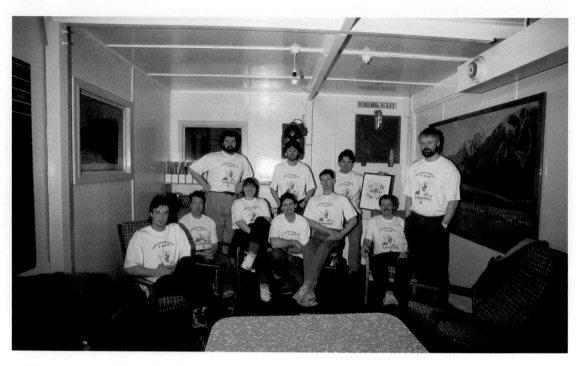

The team poses with South Pole Expedition 1958 (TAE) T-shirts in the TAE hut in the middle of winter

maintenance of the entire base and plant and new building projects.

As winter manager my ride is proving easy, with an extremely well motivated and generally mature and tolerant group. My energies can be directed into other issues: maintaining morale, dreaming up a variety of social activities, routines, the ceaseless preparation of monthly reports for Christchurch, and writing meaningful monthly newsletters for families and friends at home.

Routine is well established. The whole team continues dining together three times daily, we all work the same hours, and most are continuing to exercise regularly. As a result, insomnia is not presenting a significant problem.

Most of the team have personal projects or 'food for the mind' to avert boredom. One of interest is Joe's mind-extending development of a prototype internal combustion engine. As one of the more novel projects John utilises many Bumper Bars, now rancid and destined for the incinerator, as building blocks for a 2.5m-tall replica of his home city Palmerston North's art-deco clock tower.

Allowing problems to proceed unchecked can be unwise and my easy ride comes to an abrupt halt one Saturday morning early in June.

During smoko John and I begin debating the selection of Lotto numbers and things get out of hand somewhat. Our usual hearty verbal sparring quickly takes on argumentative proportions and continues for more than an hour.

Initially I put down to winter's intellectual inertia the reason that I cannot convince John that 1, 2, 3, 4, 5 and 6 have as much chance as any other combination, and that lucky numbers do not exist. It soon becomes apparent that my argument is not being heard because for John the debate becomes a vehicle to vent his frustrations at my management style. Since February he has been tolerant of what he sees as my failure to involve him as deputy winter manager in a management team.

PETER HARDING: 'MEDI-VAC', WINTER 1991

On 2 May I spoke to Sally White, our winter-over GD (domestic) and first-aider – a very understanding person. Symptoms of a recurring bowel infection had been brewing for a couple of weeks and I had been ignoring them, hoping they would go away.

Sally spoke to Dr Robert McFarland at McMurdo's medical clinic and he asked to see me immediately. I got the message while I was working up at Arrival Heights. On the way back to Scott Base I called in at McMurdo, where Dr McFarland wanted to keep me in overnight on a drip. I convinced him I would be okay at Scott Base, but I was worried.

What I wouldn't have believed then was that in a month's time I'd be flying back to Christchurch on a special 'medi-vac' mercy flight.

Dr McFarland's efforts were to no avail when the infection refused to respond to available treatment. My health was declining.

Friday, 21 May 1991 rates as one of the saddest days of my life. I went to McMurdo's medical clinic and was admitted, never to return to Scott Base. All those things I was going to do, all those special places I wanted to visit and special moments I would have

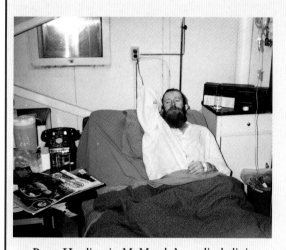

Peter Harding in McMurdo's medical clinic

photographed were no longer possible. I felt terrible; a sense of letting down the team.

Everyone at Scott Base and many from McMurdo visited me regularly, providing reassurance and keeping my spirits up. The story of the Russian doctor who had to remove his own appendix was recounted and made me appreciate the excellent attentions of Dr McFarland and his team.

[On 1 May 1961 Dr Leoni Rogozov at the Soviet base Novolazarevskaya had had to remove his own appendix when severe storm made it impossible for a rescue plane to fly in from their main base, Mirny. His assistants (the station's meteorologist and mechanic) treated the area and inserted the stitches. Rogozov dozed off and a week later he was up walking.]

After specialist consultation, New Zealand's programme made an official request to the NSF for assistance. Planning for the first midwinter landing at McMurdo since 1964 took four days.

By 4 June, the day of my flight, I was excited at the thought of going home to the green of New Zealand and getting this episode over with.

The LC-130 Hercules left Christchurch at 0545 and landed at Williams Field at 1328 – the moon was high enough to provide ground definition. The runway had been prepared for 24 hours prior to the landing, with large-wheeled vehicles dragging large chains to break up and flatten snowdrifts. After 90 minutes on the ground for refuelling, at -31°C, I was loaded aboard and we departed at 1458, arriving in Christchurch at 2315.

Lots of TV cameras and journalists were waiting at the airport, along with DSIR Antarctic Division staff and of course my partner, Nicky.

I'm happy to say that after a few ups and downs my health in 1996 is much better. I'm thankful that the Americans decided to write off the cost of this flight as a humanitarian gesture.

Our Myers Briggs character typing produced similar profiles with strong leadership abilities, with John's character extroverted and mine introverted. The extroverted leadership approach, being more openly expressive, tends towards verbalising what will happen, whereas the introverted approach, being more reticent, works on setting an example and assuming it will be followed. The introvert tends towards independence and can overlook signs and signals. The extrovert, by contrast, must be seen to lead.

John's involvement in a structured base management team during summer came to a halt when I adopted my consensus approach in February. With this, the whole group discusses issues and arrives at decisions during Saturday's base meetings, a philosophy that effectively dispenses with the need for a management team and shuts John out of the action. If a decision has to be made for the team, which is hardly ever, it is usually by way of a majority decision. Most seem happy with this arrangement.

Time is a slow healer. John and I keep our distance for a number of weeks, which causes further discomfort. It's hard sitting close together at the dinner table and avoiding eye contact.

At this time, with the airdrop approaching, a decision needs to be made on who will go off base to watch and who will stay. Gill innocently suggests we draw straws. In light of recent events I counter-suggest via e-mail that lottery-type selection, with its winners and losers, would not be a good idea. I feel it's better to strive for consensus, seeking volunteers to remain behind. If this still produces a stalemate, the decision would be based on merit. Longer term, there are more winners that way.

A swift resolution is called for as this dilemma is affecting the team and it's my responsibility to sort these things out. It's difficult confronting the truth and resolving conflict when your own actions have contributed to the problem. Good conflict resolution involves taking an honest look at yourself, hearing things you mightn't want to, listening as well as talking. John and I start after lunch and have to be reminded it's time for dinner.

This incredibly taxing and valuable learning process sees some middle ground reached on the issue of management. There is considerable relief all round and a pretty respectable friendship is back on track.

Leadership styles do vary. Scott's expedition was a Royal Navy one and his leadership was based on rank. All orders were posted as notices signed 'Captain Scott – Royal Navy'. Scott's 1910-13 expedition was segregated, with packing cases dividing the hut: officers at one end (the wardroom), and men at the kitchen end.

Shackleton's expedition was Merchant Navy and, possibly also because of his stronger charismatic personality, a more libertarian approach was taken.

Roald Amundsen dictated. His clash with his most experienced team member, Johansen, was of classic proportions. A simmering conflict between the two, based on leadership issues, erupted explosively as a result of poor communication and possibly Amundsen's poor judgment. Following the spat, Amundsen immediately evicted Johansen from the polar party and effectively never spoke to him again.

John and I certainly weren't breaking new ground. I'd like to think I'm more of a Shackleton than

Happier times with John

Left: An offering of hydroponic lettuce. Right: My Hagar birthday cake.

an Amundsen, but in light of my Norse heritage, reddish beard and consequent Antarctic nickname of 'Hagar the Horrible' (or just 'Horrible' for short), maybe I'm more of an Amundsen than I imagine. Whatever, I'm not a Scott.

There's a notice stuck on the carpenter's door at the eastern end of the base: 'Don't Slam the F--ken Door'. The three regular users of the door are Scotty, Tom and me. The prevailing north-east winds catch this exposed door if it's let go, and the resultant reverberations in the carpenter's shop pass through to Dave's work area. It irritates the hell out of him as he is the one who maintains the door seals.

Dave is a man of few words but his frustration builds to the point of posting the note. Admittedly, he did raise the issue once at a meeting earlier in the winter. Now, with our newly-honed conflict-resolution skills, the situation is resolved.

14

WINFLY

Scott Base, Scott Base, this is One Ton Camp, One Ton Camp on 5400, how copy? Over.'
No reply.

'Scott Base, Scott Base, this is One Ton Camp, One Ton Camp, do you copy? Over.' Richard Struthers, speaking softly, disguises his voice.

Mystified, Scotty eventually replies, drawing his words, 'Yeeessss, Onnneee, Tooonnn, Caaammmppp, Scotta Base, Scotta Base, we read you, over.'

International Darts on Ice and this mysterious station has come up on 5400kHz. One Ton Camp? Could it be those Aussies? For once Scotty is thrown. Other stations equally have no idea.

A GPS location is requested. Peter (Jock) Walton proceeds to read the location noted on the wall, doing his best to disguise his thick Scottish accent. Suspicions are aroused. But we insist we're a bona fide darts team, established in 1912. The One Ton Camp bit begins to fall into place. Our best player has gone out and not returned, we add, after saying, 'I'm just going outside, and may be some time.' Even the Aussies understand now.

At the A-frame, on the same ice shelf where Scott's party perished, One Ton Camp joins tonight's game of 501. We're permitted to stand closer than regulation distance from the board to offset the disadvantage of low light – tilley lamp and head lamps. Casey wins.

We're at the A-frame on an AFT course. The darts game doubles as a worthwhile HF radio exercise.

The first vestiges of the sun's return are noticed on 17 July, while Joe, Tom and I are on Observation Hill on a JASART stretcher-lowering exercise. It's -39.6°C with 15-20 knot winds. Cold. We're high on an exposed ridge using only light finger-gloves for rope-work and our fingers quickly numb. Little time is spent marvelling at the light.

Ten days later when I'm outside for the 0900 met obs the north-east is illuminated with curtains of red and yellow.

A few more days and our JASART team make first-light trips to the Erebus Glacier Tongue to check the new sea ice. Some nacreous clouds are observed, but they're no more than the less than impressive aurorae seen during winter.

Then less than a month later, after days of cloud, the solar orb is sighted from Crater Hill on 27 August. Now into September, our last month here, each day is rapidly lengthening.

The Winfly operation's 10 ski-equipped LC-130 Hercules flights from Christchurch run with little disruption.

Due to the cold, LC-130 Hercs keep their engines running while on the ground at Williams Field at Winfly

112

Top: The moon rising over Ross Ice Shelf, Jan at right. Bottom: Dramatic end-of-winter colour.

Our final six weeks until October (the Winfly period) is the transition leading up to, and allows preparations for, the next season's summer. Our insulated existence is coming to an end.

McMurdo's population doubles to almost 500 at Winfly so the notion of a Ross Island winter community also comes to an end and we function as two programmes again.

Four days before Winfly's first landing 40 from McMurdo joined us for dinner to acknowledge winter's passing. Winter friends from McMurdo continue to be welcome; it's the newer faces who are generally kept more at arm's length.

However, the new Scott Base faces are welcome. Carpenters Jock and Richard are here to renovate part of the Hatherton Laboratory and build some new sleeping accommodation in Q Hut. Ecologists Ian Hawes and Anna Schwarz, and ozone specialist Stevo Wood return to continue ongoing science programmes. NZAP staff Gill, Peter and new programme support officer Rex Hendry visit for a few days. We feel sane enough not to insist that our new arrivals 'bear only small gifts, and not big boots'. They immediately slot into our routine.

Scotty visits his father, flying out on the first turn-around flight on 20 August and returning five days later.

Our fridge is bursting with freshies as we've been treated to an extra dose. And it's good to have some more wine, especially red.

TONY BROMLEY: A SECOND WINTER AT VANDA

Late in January 1974 the last helicopter departed, leaving a final box of fresh food and the well wishes of the crew, and taking our last letters to loved ones in New Zealand. Our only contact with the outside world for the next nine months would be the six-hourly meteorological radio reports to Scott Base.

With feelings of trepidation, the four of us moved slowly back to the simple buildings, our home for the rest of the year: a main living hut, 7m x 4m, with the sleeping area separated from the rest of the single room by a black curtain, the 6m x 3m laboratory and a small food storage shed.

There were no bathing or showering facilities – a weekly scrub-down over a tin basin was to be sufficient for personal hygiene. And the outside toilet, 100m away, was a 44-gallon drum with a wooden seat in a chilly, door-less 'sentry-box', but with a great view of the Olympus range.

Private corners were established in the laboratory crammed with instruments and tools for maintaining 10 or so scientific programmes. In spite of the lack of space we never felt really cramped. Science, the maintenance of the power supply and communications equipment and domestic chores kept us busy. Mutual assistance was crucial and fortunately we were a very harmonious group. Fire-watch and cooking duties were shared on a week-on, week-off roster.

Tony Bromley

Kerosene lamps were used for lighting to save precious battery power: a 12-volt DC battery bank, kept charged by a wind-powered generator and auxiliary diesel engine, powered the base.

Cooking became quite competitive, especially bread-making. Anyone guilty of producing a 'flat' loaf could expect several days of friendly 'rubbishing'. Food variety was limited and great efforts were made to produce meals 'with a difference'. Other than basics like bulk flour, tea and coffee, ingredients were limited to a small variety of dehydrated (dehy) or frozen vegetables (carrots, peas, onions and potatoes) and assorted frozen cuts of meat. Frozen foods was simply stacked outside until needed.

Water was our most precious commodity – every litre measured as a cost in effort and diesel fuel. Ice was chipped by hand from the surface of Lake Vanda then carried up to the station's ice melter. Our total daily water use was restricted to 40 litres for all drinking, cooking and washing.

Heating inside the hut was limited and the temperature up to a metre above the floor was only 10-15°C warmer than outside. We sometimes used to sit on chairs placed up on the tables where the warmer air had risen!

Meteorology was the main science programme and in those days, before automatic stations and data loggers, the 'satellite' screens scattered throughout the valley had to be visited every 10 days to change charts and reset instruments. This involved trekking up to 190km a week summer and winter. Venturing outside required careful dressing and planning. To save weight little survival equipment was carried on these trips (against Antarctic Division rulings). A dehy meat bar or two, water in a thermos and a sleeping bag were the norm. No radios were taken: the so-called portable models of that era still weighed 25lb.

Travel in the winter was generally surprisingly easy – the moon would light the valley brilliantly, and at other times the darkness of the sky was so intense that navigation by starlight was perfectly feasible. We always feared being caught in a surprise violent storm with up to 180 km/h winds which could have proved fatal. Even a simple fall resulting in a broken leg, if you were hours from base, could have had deadly consequences.

One midwinter trip took Haggis (Peter Thompson) and myself to Don Juan Pond, west of Vanda to take samples for Dr Tetsuya Torii of the Japan Polar Institute. A year or two earlier Japanese scientists had discovered a new mineral never before found in its natural state – calcium chloride hexahydrate, or what they named 'antarcticite'. The pond had never been know to freeze. We were to see what state the pond was at the coldest time of the year. And at -63°C the pond was still liquid. Perhaps the antarcticite was keeping the water from freezing? Samples were taken and at the end of the year sent to Japan, but I never learned whether the mineral was the key to this unique phenomenon.

Midwinter was marked by a four-man banquet of dehy food and a few drinks from our tiny supply of liquor. Finally in early September the first glow of the returning sun was visible to the east and a trip up the southern wall of the valley gave us our first direct sight of the sun in seven months. Tucked away in this east/west lying valley, our winter was longer.

The last weeks at Vanda were frantic, preparing scientific records for sending to New Zealand and spring cleaning the base before our replacements for the next summer season arrived.

As we watched to the east for the first glimpse of the helicopter that would end our isolation, I felt a mixture of relief and sadness – relief that all four of us had survived a most remarkable and dangerous winter, and sadness that a challenging and absorbing part of my life was soon to end. And the feeling that I would never come back to this wonderfully unique place.

[During the winters of 1969, 1970, and 1974, three small teams wintered over at Vanda Station to collect scientific data. Tony Bromley doesn't elaborate on what made him return in 1974 as team leader for a second winter, after his 1970 visit. As a research meteorologist, Tony has also made five shorter visits to Antarctica.]

The sun, freshies, new faces and heightened activity add a breath of fresh air. Frigid temperatures also accompany this period, but we don't drop below our record -49.6°C, recorded on 2 May. It's all downhill, full speed, to the end of our year.

Ian and Anna's Winfly programme is particularly bold, continuing K081's ecological investigations at Lake Vanda. The Americans are operating helicopters to the Taylor Valley during Winfly, supporting their long-term ecological research programme. Ian and Anna can share helicopter support seldom offered at this colder time of the year.

While I'm on the ice fall with Jock and Richard on AFT the sound of a Huey certainly heralds the approach of summer. Jim, with Tom in support, flies on the first mission, bringing up Channel Five's VHF repeater on Mt Newall. This is needed for communications into Lake Vanda.

They're plucked off before completing their task. During Winfly, with its short window of daylight each day and the cold, helicopters are required for safety reasons to fly in tandem. On this mission one develops a fault, so both machines have to return. Jim will make another trip.

During final preparations with Ian and Anna at Scott Base, John's team further highlights the potential problems with operating machinery at below -40°C. Vehicles plugged in at Scott Base are always

Joe searching for the spark-plugs

TOM HOPKINS

IAN HAWES

TOM HOPKINS

KO81 at Vanda, Winfly 1995: Tent camp on lake ice (top); Anna Schwarz with frozen Jim Beam, and attending to science (below).

kept warm and are easy to start. But you notice the effects of cold when you drive away – extra revs are required to break the toffee-like lubricants in the drive mechanisms and the friction soon gets these systems flowing.

The four-wheel motorbike at Vanda, with no block heater, will be hard to warm and could take hours to start. The bike is intended for commuting between the living quarters at Vanda's new refuge hut and the sampling site near the other end of the lake. A generator will be required at each site.

I suggest that if Ian and Anna were to live in tents at the sampling site this would eliminate the need for both the motorbike and a second generator. The Ross Dependency Research Committee approves this altered plan as it further reduces the likelihood of environmental impact.

Keep things simple is good advice in Antarctica. Machines work well at Vanda during the summer, and with little recent experience of working there during winter it's easy to understand how the original plan evolved. It's hard to appreciate the rigours of field conditions when you're drawing up plans in the comfort of an office at home.

Tom takes on the responsibility of logistical support for the event. His field support role and close liaison with Robin at Helo Ops at McMurdo makes him the logical choice.

Once the Americans have their Taylor Valley camps established, Ian and Anna are ready to fly. But first Tom, Dave and Joe fly ahead to set up camp and the generators (a standby generator is taken in to cover breakdowns).

The cold certainly affects their work. Tents that need tensioning of the fabric when inserting poles (conventional alpine-style dome or tunnel tents) are hard to erect in the cold. The fabric becomes so stiff and brittle it can easily rip. Two classic Antarctic pre-assembled, four-poled, pyramid-shaped polar tents, which are folded out then pegged down, are easy to pitch and each is fastened to the bullet-

proof lake ice with 15 ice screws. This should withstand the fiercest of Dry Valley winds.

A hut was flown to the sampling site at the end of last summer and fastened down to large anchors. It hasn't moved during the winter so should continue to hold.

Emergency food and equipment are stored at Vanda's refuge hut as a back-up.

Ian and Anna fly in and Dave and Joe return to base. For the next three days temperatures at Lake Vanda hover around -48°C, causing two generator malfunctions. Joe has to fly out with new generators, eating into valuable helicopter time.

Freshwater ice is harder when it's colder. The hand auger used during summer doesn't work well, but Ian and Anna's revolutionary probe ice-melter rips through the four metres and sampling can begin.

Ian and Anna make five trips over five weeks, with interludes at Scott Base where they warm up and use the Crary Lab to investigate their samples. Tom supports the first trip, Bruce the second, but with the temperatures rising and generators running smoothly Ian and Anna's last three visits are unsupported.

Surprisingly, deep lake temperatures of +25°C are found, similar to summertime readings, although it's cooler at shallower levels. The algal population in the DCM also remains at similar levels to last summer, and photosynthesis is evident as soon as the sun returns, albeit at lower levels initially.

Stevo's ongoing ozone work continues, mostly conducted from the Arrival Heights laboratory. Stevo's interests involve measuring the stratospheric trace gases active in ozone depletion chemistry.

Stevo suffers a mechanical malfunction that could have been quite serious. He is returning from the Heights, quietly coasting down the hill before turning into Scott Base, when the front wheel of his Toyota falls off. Joe had fitted the wheel in the garage at

Top: On Crater Hill for my first view of the returning sun. Bottom: Scott's hut beautifully cloaked in snow.

+20°C, then put the vehicle straight out into -40°C, whereupon the alloy rim contracted and loosened the wheel nuts. Loose wheel nuts eventually fall off.

Jan, Joe, Richard, Sean, Scotty and I, along with McMurdo doctor Randall Hyer and Joe's friend Gail Noton, experience our share of cold when we camp out on a fam trip to Cape Evans.

The route to the Erebus Glacier Tongue has been flagged in recent weeks and the sastrugi experienced on the reconnaissance trips early in August have been scraped off by machine. Past the EGT, new season's sea ice without any major cracks affords quick travel to Scott's hut at Evans.

The hut is beautifully cloaked in a mantle of winter snow and weak sunlight extends soft-tone lighting. The door needs clearing before we can get in and with the extreme cold and darkness inside, and snow covering the windows, the sombre mood is pronounced. Building cloud obscures the sun to the north-west and extends a beautiful yellow sunset.

We pitch tents near the emergency refuge hut, where the eight of us cram inside for cups of steaming mulled wine and hot pasta and vegetables to help counter the cold. Outside, at -40°C, the continual hum of a generator ruins the tranquillity as it powers the block heater on H-28.

Sleep comes easily later, despite the cold and noise.

On waking we find that our moist breath has condensed on and dampened the narrow openings of our 'mummy' sleeping bags. Ian and Anna have been having this problem at Vanda, especially after a number of days. They have no drying facilities at their camp so they take fresh bags on each trip.

By the time breakfast and packing are complete the Barne Glacier has disappeared behind cloud, ruling out our continuing to Royds. We retreat in deteriorating visibility to the flags at the EGT and the American camp, where an author and an artist are ensconced. A visit guarantees a hot drink.

Camped at Cape Evans

119

Castle Rock against a yellow sky

The NSF funds an Artists' and Writers' Programme that allows artists, photographers and writers the opportunity to interpret this wonderful place. Briton Sarah Wheeler spent time at both McMurdo and Scott Base last summer and has returned to work on her book *Terra Incognita*. This location has also inspired American artist Lucia Deleiris. The form and light here at this time of year is the stuff artists' dreams are made of.

Light reflecting off Scott Base

Two weeks before the opening flight for 1995-96, scheduled for 3 October, our work rates increase a notch or two. Winter works programmes are virtually complete and our end-of-season reports are well under way.

With one week to go, Tom, Scotty's brother, phones with news that their father has died. A mixture of sadness and relief clouds the final week for Scotty, and for many of the rest of the team. Scotty won't have to face his dad's suffering again; the last visit had been tough enough.

Gill arranges for Telecom to organise a tele-conference link to the funeral at St Peter's Anglican church at Mt Maunganui. Friends comfort Scotty during Reverend Geoff Crawshaw's moving service. Technology allows Scotty to share a precious moment in his life, from a distance of over 4500km.

15

A Big Totara has Fallen

We sit in the choir stalls of St Peter's at Mt Maunganui. It's 6 July 1996 and Reverend Geoff Crawshaw's voice again comforts. For Dave, Jan, John, Sean and me tears flow freely, as they do for the rest of the congregation, including Dan, Gazza, Graham and Scott, our summer friends.

Hope bravely delivers an emotive and superbly composed eulogy to Scotty, the man with whom she'd found true love. He lies in front of us, in a hideous matt-finished, light brown metal casket embellished with chrome adornment.

Hope refers to the casket as 'the Cadillac'. It doesn't suit Scotty but there hadn't been time to find something appropriate.

Scotty had arrived in the United States 10 days earlier, intending to spend the summer with Hope. He caught up with his friend Maddison and headed to Telluride in Colorado for some long-planned parapenting.

Flying was Scotty's passion. He went to 16,000ft without oxygen on the morning of 29 June and, full of pride, went up again that afternoon. His canopy collapsed during an aerobatic manoeuvre in the low-density air and he fell 75ft to the ground.

Hasty preparations have bought Scotty home for the last time.

Scotty's son Dane attempts to say a few words but finds the occasion too overwhelming.

Scotty's family has had more than its share of tragedy. His mother died in a car crash in 1979, his father died last September and brother Tom had a brush with death when his fire engine crashed near Taupo last November. Tom has one remaining family

Scotty

member, brother Geoff. Tom, determined to recover and having progressed from a wheelchair to crutches with one leg heavily calipered, struggles forward to eulogise. He praises Scotty for his unstinting support, especially during his recovery at the Otara Spinal Unit. Scotty energised his family as he energised Scott Base.

John and I are out at the sea ice runway watching the first C-141 touch down. We're wearing our Sorrels, well-worn jeans and slightly soiled jackets unzipped and our faces are pasty and grey with stubble.

Malcolm, the first Senzrep for summer 1995-96, disembarks with seven new winter-over crew, fresh and fully wrapped.

'Good trip?' Our smiles say more.

I feel the prescribed end-of-year emotions: excitement to be going home, yet sadness. What a year it's been! My thoughts dwell on the impending three days before handover. What have I forgotten?

THE DOGGO'S DILEMMA

During my first days at Scott Base, early in November 1984, one moment remains vivid: the dog handler (doggo) for the 1983-84 season, Alasdair (Al) Roy, emotionally farewelling his dogs.

The moment was not only etched in Al's face, but was also felt keenly by those dogs not hitched up to the sledge to haul their master on his last ride – to the aeroplane. The sledge and team, with new doggo Kevin Conaglen in charge, pulled away from the front of Scott Base. The dogs remaining, straining on leashes, yelped and howled hauntingly. They certainly seemed to know.

Twelve years later Al still relates the moment as being 'pretty tough' and 'harder than farewelling my family when leaving for the ice'. The long phase of handing over to the new doggo prolonged the agony.

Al recalls the depths of winter as a time when bonds became stronger; if he had departed during summer his feelings wouldn't have been the same. 'Feeding them in the dark and when the weather was rough was the time they seemed most happy to see me. This appreciation was reward for my efforts.' Only in the worst of weather were they brought inside.

Al, who sells real estate in Queenstown, now has only one dog, labrador Abbe, named after one of Scott Base's huskies.

Al Roy and the huskies. The Scott Base huskies were removed from Antarctica in February 1987 for economic and environmental reasons. No dogs remain on the continent.

Top: A C-5 Galaxy lands on the sea ice runway against the backdrop of the Royal Society Range.
Below: The huge C-5 about to unload.

These days are a blur as two teams vie for space and time.

New chef Stewart Hopkins, Scotty's replacement, has big kitchen clogs to fill. I feel sorry for Stewart, who'll be judged by the first meal he serves. It's a tough call for a chef, whose performance is judged at least twice each day.

I find it hard to contemplate what it would be like to stay on with this new group, but Bruce is doing just that as he's been asked to remain for a month and assist with some Cape Roberts Project preparations.

Gill arrives mid-afternoon, in time for handover. It's third time lucky for me as I get to take Bruce the Gnome to the flagpole. I lower our New Zealand flag from the base's pole at 1700 on Friday 6 October 1995 and Malcolm raises his – 240 days after our roles were reversed at the start of winter. Only two stars remain on our wind-frayed flag.

I relinquish my position, which included the responsibilities as Justice of the Peace and Coroner of the Ross Dependency, and feel thankful neither role was called upon.

Jan, John and Scotty fly home the following day; John reminds us that it's his 369th day on ice.

The rest, minus Bruce and Jim, who is completing a longer handover, fly home on Monday. Most of the base respectfully assembles down at the bottom entrance to farewell us; we're on the receiving end this time. At 1530 the large freezer-style door is nudged open for us for the last time.

'Gawd, it's cold, where's my jacket?' Stepping out into a drizzly southerly convinces us that it doesn't matter where you are – a cold day is a cold day. By 2200 it's dark at Christchurch airport.

When I returned during the height of summer during the 1980s we were welcomed by the smell of vegetation well before landing. This time it's different but it's not too cold to get a good whiff of life as we step outside the Starlifter.

Lowering our winter 1995 flag – our year has finished

Only Sean and I are not otherwise occupied at the Windsor Private Hotel, our programme's Christchurch home away from home, so we head into town. First we check out the grass in Cranmer Square. I recall in 1986 when the winter-overs arrived home and went a little troppo rolling around on the grass. We are a little more reserved and are happy just to touch it.

'Watch that dog turd, Sean!'

A recent issue of *The Press* has rated Phloyds in the Square one of the best cafe bars. Hip-looking clientele, predominantly in their early twenties, contrast with what we've been used to. Have we been in a time-warp? McMurdo regulars at Scott Base's bar are predominantly in their thirties, with some quadragenarian Vietnam/Woodstock relics making an impact.

The prices certainly indicate a time-warp too: we haven't had to fork out cash for food for a year!

Reunited with Liz at Queenstown

Better than the Parkroyal, a couple of nights in an ex-New Zealand Forest Service hut at Stafford Bay

After paying a dollar a can or a dollar a nip, we're reluctant to part with too much.

'Where's the tambourine, Sean?' Scott Base has a tambourine on the bar in which McMurdo guests leave their greenbacks.

The Windsor's characteristic morning call, a jangle played on a small xylophone, is followed by a cheery voice announcing, 'breakfast is ready'. It's a sound we last heard just over a year ago, just before leaving for the ice.

There's no distant hum of a generator, but there's been a constant din outside our window for an hour or two. Morning traffic swishes past around Cranmer Square on the one-way system and the tyre sound suggests it's raining.

The window reveals a gloomy day – a cluttered landscape of urban congestion. We feel claustrophobic after open horizons, simplicity and grandeur. Those pedestrians walking past – if only they knew!

Disappointing is the lack of green visual stimulation on this grey wet morning. The whole spectrum of green is enhanced after a long absence.

A day is spent at the office, checking in bags of issue clothing and again putting faces to the voices we've been familiar with for a year. We farewell John, who's about to fly to Wellington to meet Sue, without their children, Hayden and Sarah. He's apprehensive.

I'm apprehensive myself when first off the Boeing

in Queenstown the following afternoon. Liz, distinctive in her purple mohair jersey, has longer hair. Our long-overdue hug is prolonged and firm. The Deux Cheveux (Citroen 2CV) waits in the carpark.

I'd read in an in-flight magazine that the Boardwalk Seafood Restaurant in Queenstown's new Steamer Wharf Village gets the thumbs up. We're not driving home to Clyde tonight; we've got a year's catching up to start.

Home. Our half-acre with its year's extra growth is impressive, especially with spring's flush with flowering plants and shrubs. And it's a pleasure to walk around in a T-shirt and without gloves or hat.

Liz's interior decorating receives 100 per cent approval. The joint account has been well used during the year away. At least the feature wall in our lounge is still free for yesterday's impulse purchase in Christchurch: a large framed watercolour of five emperor penguins.

If home is where the heart is then Clyde is not. The other side of Haast Pass and an indulgence of green beckons. With a light pack, but without Antarctica's encumbrance of extra clothing and equipment, we leave our car at Jackson's Bay. A leaden sky promises a wetting before we'll make it to Stafford River and it delivers. Thrashing through piles of beech windfall, brought down by heavy snows during winter, provides a novel distant-remembered

Liz paddling on Okarito Lagoon

experience, as does wearing no raincoat in a warm north-west rain.

We cross the Stafford's rising waters, arriving at the humble six-bunk ex-New Zealand Forest Service Stafford Hut half an hour before dark. It's all ours. We have a driftwood fire blazing by the time the rain turns to real West Coast proportions and drums on the corrugated-iron roof. Candlelight and a good Aussie red from our favourite chipped enamel tramping cups add to our comfort.

Early during our year at Scott Base the plan had always been a night in Christchurch's Parkroyal after a limousine trip from the airport, but the idea lost momentum along the way. It couldn't compare with this.

Heavy surf at high tide pounds on the steep pebbly beach. It reminds me of when Scotty and I spent our afternoon at Cape Bird's beach. There are sandflies instead of young Adelies here. We spend a day loitering on the thin coastal strip of Stafford Bay, between a wild ocean and wild thickly-matted coastal vegetation.

Nature still rules here on the Coast, just as it does in Antarctica. Rusted crayfish pots, pieces of rope and plastic buoys are thrown very high up the beach, along with large driftwood logs.

A day's paddling on the Okarito Lagoon is another magic Coast experience. The lagoon's layered backdrop – water, a strip of flax groves, tall trunks and canopy of kahikatea forest backed by the Southern Alps – equals the grandeur of the Royal Society Range. The summits of Mt Tasman and Mt Cook are heavily cloaked in snow: I'm surprised that snow still holds an attraction.

We spot a few white herons, plenty of stilts and ducks, but no godwits have arrived at the lagoon yet. An honest paddle home into a brisk south-west wind takes us to quaint Okarito village.

A big driftwood fire is a must at the old Okarito Youth Hostel, a converted single-room school. Macri Tackett, a chef from McMurdo's galley, has taken my advice and has been here for most of a week.

My first day back at Hubbards Pharmacy in Alexandra I have to think twice about dispensing my first prescription. But half an hour later a number of familiar faces have visited and it's back on autopilot.

In a bar after Scotty's funeral we sit with backs to the television. The All Blacks are thrashing the Aussies (revenge for the darts) in a wet test in Wellington, but we are more interested in reflecting on our year one ice, and life during the nine months since. Generally, unsettledness has prevailed.

Jan spent summer at Fox Glacier with Alpine Guides and is now at the International Antarctic Centre in Christchurch.

Engineers Dave and John are both back in Palmerston North. Dave feels he's only now settling back at Palmerston North's hospital and John now has job number two – commuting to Pahiatua's Tui Dairy Factory. Uncertainty clouds his future with Tui's proposed merger with another dairy company.

Sean had a short stint at the Government Communications Security Bureau at Waihopai, followed Christine to Sydney and dabbled in some work there, then convinced Christine to return to Wellington and is looking for work in the capital himself.

Bruce is back in Dunedin with his previous employer but is generally still contemplating the future.

Jim is somewhere in Wellington, keeping a low profile.

Joe and Gail announced their engagement before leaving Antarctica, spent summer working in Wanaka, married in Colorado in April and are presently travelling in Alaska, unaware of Scotty's death. Rumour has it they won't settle in the States but will return to Wanaka.

Tom has dabbled with stints of work in the Southern Alps, and has travelled thousands of miles in the States skiing and visiting many McMurdo friends. He's back in New Zealand working at the Craigieburn Ski Field.

Liz and I have sold up in Clyde. We both applied for 1996-97 at Scott Base but Ange and Mess from winter 1994 pipped us. A subsequent job at Kaikoura pharmacy only lasted two months before I headed for Christchurch.

Scotty, arguably the most restless of our team, is finally at rest. Maybe this is the catalyst our team needs.

Our Scott Base experience was like a return to childhood: full-on adventure with hardly a care in the world. All our basic needs were provided for: a comfortable and clean home, food on the table, entertainment, company and routine. The parameters of life were limited. We enjoyed financial security with accumulating bank balances and few bills, and were faced with few day-to-day decisions.

The question we are most asked has been: 'What's it like to be back in civilisation?'

Where's civilisation?

Mt Maunganui has a restaurant called Restless Waters, an appropriate place to meet others there for dinner.

'Hey, let's get a Lotto ticket, you guys,' Sean suggests with a mischievous grin and in anticipation of a response from John and me. We giggle. Sean wants more than a lucky dip: he selects 1, 2, 3, 4, 5 and 6, along with other combinations.

The sudden loss of Scotty, a key component of our successful year, has quantified the bonds forged during our year on ice.

'Ka hinga te totara o te wao nui a Tane.' When the Maori lose a prominent member of society they equate it to the falling of the totara tree in the great forest of Tane. Scotty was a big totara in our forest.

Scotty's dream was to fly off Observation Hill – an illegal activity.
Did he or didn't he?

APPENDICES

Appendix One

THE 1994-95 SUMMER SCIENCE PROGRAMME

FIELD SCIENCE

Event K001: Cape Roberts Project (Preparations)

Jim Cowie and Alex Pyne.

Six countries are involved in this ongoing geological drilling project over the next two or three years. It rates as one of New Zealand's most ambitious Antarctic science events since International Geophysical Year (1957-58) by drilling off Cape Roberts, with a rig sited on the sea ice, two 400m cores of seabed sediments will be taken over two summers, sea ice permitting.

These Ross Sea sedimentary rocks, estimated to be 30-100 million years old, will throw light on a number of issues: climatic history, the existence of ice sheets and an indication of the time and tectonic setting when rifting was initiated, resulting in the formation of the Transantarctic Mountains.

During 1994-95 preparations included checking sea ice movement monitoring systems and off-loading 250 tonnes of equipment from the Italian programme's vessel, *Italica*, at Cape Roberts.

Event K012: Ecology of Antarctic Fish

John Macdonald, Clive Evans, Victor Cauty, Robyn Holland, Nick Ling, Craig Thorburn and Bruce Anderson.

Auckland University's biological group continued investigating the anatomical, physiological and biochemical specialisations in Antarctic fish that allow them to survive in water close to freezing.

Bruce, a co-recipient of the RDRC Science Award (designed to attract young scientists to Antarctic research), investigated the effect of Scott Base's sewage discharge on the local marine environment. He found that the impact is localised.

Event K022: Antarctic Moss Genetic Variation

Dieter Adam, Pat Selkirk (Australia) and Tracy Dale, with Warren Herrick (field support).

Expanding on work in 1992-93, Waikato University bryologists visited numerous sites and used a minimum-impact sampling strategy to collect material to study the genetic variation in selected mosses, the predominant form of terrestrial vegetation in Antarctica.

Event K024: Photosynthesis in Antarctic Moss and Lichens

Allan Green, Rod Seppelt (Australia), Ludgar Kappen and Burkhardt Schroeter (Germany), Kadmiel Maseyk.

This Waikato University event, with international collaboration, studied the photosynthetic performance of lichens and mosses in the field at Granite Harbour.

This work established a base-line for use as an environmental indicator. Ozone depletion increases ultraviolet B rays and hinders photosynthesis, while increased carbon dioxide production (the greenhouse effect) enhances photosynthesis.

This team measured photosynthesis at -20°C, a record low value for field measurement.

Event K025: Thermophilic Bacteria

Hugh Morgan, Juergen Wiegel and Karl Stetter (Germany), with Rachel Brown and Warren Herrick (field support).

Thermophilic (heat-loving) bacteria found in Antarctic's volcanic hot spots are some of the most isolated and the least affected by human contact. This third Waikato University (and German) project sampled the heated ground on Mt Erebus and Mt Melbourne for new strains and discovered several.

Event K044: Geophysical Investigation of Transantarctic Mountain Front

Ron Hackney, Tony Haver and Julie Quinn, with Bill Atkinson (field support).

This Victoria University geophysical event revisited the Nimrod Glacier area of the Ross Ice Shelf, 500km south of Scott Base, to follow up work investigated in 1990-91.

Radio-echo sounding, geomagnetic and gravity measurement techniques were used to investigate the earth's crustal structure below the ice, at the boundary between East and West Antarctica. This work further tested the belief that the rifting uplift of the Transantarctic Mountains (the boundary between the East and West Antarctic plates) was achieved by a simple geological shear mechanism.

Event K045: Gondwanaland Movement in Polar Region and Diatom Studies

David Christofel, Adam Wooler and Nerida Bleakley, with Rachel Brown (field support).

This Victoria University event supplemented earlier work on the edge of the Polar Plateau. Samples were examined to study the direction of the earth's magnetic field in Beacon sedimentary mud-stones laid down 200-400 million years ago (a study known as palaeomagnetism).

When related to similar rocks in South America, Africa, India, Australia and New Zealand, which were believed to make up the super-continent Gondwanaland, this helps to determine the breakup of Gondwanaland with respect to the magnetic pole and latitude. For the most part, results have been conflicting.

Nerida, the other recipient of the RDRC's Science Award, sampled two sites for glacial deposits containing microfossil diatoms. These could point to the existence of marine basins inland of the Transantarctic Mountains three million years ago.

Event K057: Circulatory Physiology of Antarctic Fish

Bill Davidson and Malcolm Forster, Michael Axelsson and Stefan Nilsson (Sweden).

This group of Canterbury University and Swedish zoologists continued their development of a method to measure oxygen uptake across the gills of Antarctic fish, without the loss of blood from the fish. This work also allowed investigation into heart rates and physiological utilisation of oxygen at a cellular level.

Event K061: Geological Evolution of South Victoria Land

Yvonne Cook with Danny Higgins, Sean Waters and Tarn Pilkington (field support).

Yvonne from Otago University continued her PhD work unravelling the complex history of the 400-500-million-year-old Wilson Terrane mountain-belt remnants, sampling at various sites. This rock, predating Gondwanaland's breakup, is similar to rock found in western North America could record the first opening of the Pacific Ocean.

Event K063: Sperm Competition in Adelie Penguins

Fiona Hunter (Britain), Marj Wright and Rob Harcourt.

Adelie penguins generally mate at the same colony with the same partner each year. An Otago University team with Fiona from Cambridge University spent three months at Cape Bird investigating whether female birds seek out higher-quality males. The study looked at whether copulation takes place prior to re-pairing with their mate or during the time she is re-paired and whether she maintains her partner's help in raising her offspring.

Event K064: Preservation of Glaciotectonic Structures

Sean Fitzsimmons and Marcus van der Goes.

Otago University's Geography Department study spent time working on the margins of alpine glaciers in the Dry Valleys, investigating the process of glaciation and deposits left behind. This further developed field criteria that can be used specifically to interpret the deposits laid down in the Pleistocene era (one million years ago).

Event K081: Antarctic Aquatic Ecosystems

Clive Howard-Williams, Ian Hawes, Mark James, Kevin Purdy (Britain) and Pete Mason (hydrologist).

The ongoing study by the ecology division of NIWA provides information on the biology of Antarctica's inland aquatic ecosystems in the Dry Valleys.

This year's work investigated the effect of the rising level of Lake Vanda on algae populating the zone of salinity known at the Deep Chlorophyll Maximum. It showed that photo-

synthetic performance and algal populations at this 60-65m depth are holding up well.

Ian returned with Anna Schwarz at Winfly 1995 to continue work at Lake Vanda immediately after the long darkness of winter. Pete Mason conducted hydrological investigations related to measuring meltwater flow into Lake Vanda.

Event K088: Air-Snow Pollution Interaction

Tom Clarkson and Tom Kerr.

This NIWA meteorological research study over two years investigates the impact, with regard to airborne pollution, Scott Base has had/is having on its environment. Prevailing low-level air currents over Scott Base were determined this year and calculated deposit sites will be sampled for pollutants at a future date.

Event K122: Population Dynamics of Ross Island Penguin Rookeries

Peter Wilson, Brian Karl, Kerry Barton and Bruce Thomas, Nat Polish and Mike Beigel (United States).

Nelson's Landcare Research continued its ongoing studies as New Zealand's contribution to the International Survey of Antarctic Seabirds. Aerial photographic surveying and ground work helped quantify key factors in determining the success of Adelie penguin breeding.

They did not only count birds. The 'foraging effort' of adult birds returning to feed chicks, sea ice conditions affecting access to open water, breeding success and chick condition were all quantified. This work monitors any impact on penguin populations.

Event K131: The Breakup of Sea Ice

Tim Haskell, Colin Fox, Paul Callaghan, Craig Eccles, Pat Langhorne, Chris Gannon, Simon Gibson and Matthew Jury, Susan Frankenstein and Hayley Shen (United States).

This event, sponsored by Industrial Research Ltd, launched a six-year study investigating sea ice properties related to sea ice breakup. Six years' work will provide much data to help interpret: the ice's impact on southern ocean climate, how ice maintains much of its strength close to melting point, how wave motion energy is transferred to the ice and how this relates to ice breakup.

Event K141: Anaerobic Micro-organisms

Henri Kaspar and Takatoshi Nakamura.

Two microbiologists from the Cawthron Institute in Nelson went to Bratina Island to investigate 'extremeophiles', micro-organisms that survive in very cold oxygen-free conditions.

This work could be of benefit to technology, isolating new bioactive compounds and enzymes which function optimally at low temperatures. This is of particular interest to the food, chemical and pharmaceutical industries.

Event K150: Properties of Permafrost

Iain Campbell, Graeme Claridge, Dave Campbell and Roger MacCulloch.

Land and Soil Consultancy Services and Waikato University scientists worked on determining how human activities affect the Antarctic environment. Permafrost property measurement can be used to determine how the permafrost and the atmosphere interact physically and chemically in response to human activities.

HATHERTON GEOSCIENCES LABORATORY AND ARRIVAL HEIGHTS SCIENCE

(Event staff are listed if they visited during 1994-95.)

Various universities and institutes run ongoing scientific experiments at Scott Base's two laboratories. Most of this data collection continues year round and is monitored by Scott Base technicians.

Event K055: Antarctic Mesophere Ionisation

Andre von Biel, Lijia Ma, Graham Fraser and Roger Govind.

The mesophere is the 'middle atmosphere' in the lower ionosphere (60-85km above the earth). This ongoing Canterbury University study continued two experiments studying properties and dynamics of ions in this region.

This research helps in understanding the dynamics of air movement in the Antarctic mesophere. Scott Base's proximity to both the geographic South Pole and the magnetic South Pole makes this an ideal location to study certain mesophere characteristics.

Event K056: Atmospheric Corrosion of Aluminium

This long-term Canterbury University investigation is monitoring aluminium samples exposed to Antarctica's atmosphere at Scott Base (along with other sites in other countries).

Event K069: Geomagnetic Pulsations across the Polar Cap

Dave Neudegg (Australia).

Otago University and Dave's Newcastle University measure ULF (ultra low frequency) magnetic waves at five sites (four Australian Antarctic bases and Scott Base). These magnetic waves, which are propagated from the magnetosphere hundreds of kilometres out, are associated with the earth's magnetic field. This work aids investigation into the dynamics of these waves both within and through the polar cap region.

Event K085: Atmospheric (Ozone) Research

Steve Wood, Sylvia Nichol, Karin Kreher, Alan Thomas and Carlo Valenti (Italy).

This ongoing NIWA programme measures both ozone levels and the particular trace gases that are believed to contribute to ozone breakdown and formation of an ozone hole.

Dobson and Brewer spectrometers measure ozone levels in the stratosphere (17-55km above earth). The ozone hole formation peaks late in winter, so much of the research begins at Winfly.

The lowest known level of ozone was measured at 128 Dobson Units (DU) in 1993. A trend exists, with DU measures of 217, 164, 144, 143, 151, 128, 133, 130 each year respectively from 1988-95.

Event K087: Air Sampling

Every two weeks air samples are drawn into pressurised cylinders at Arrival Heights and are sent to NIWA in Welling-

ton for analysis. These samples are compared with those taken from various locations around New Zealand.

This Antarctic air, which is considered to be unpolluted, is used as a base-line for measuring pollutants such as methane and carbon monoxide. This is of value in assisting with climatic-change prediction models.

Event K089: Meteorology

Daily observations including barometric pressure, temperature, wind, and direct, diffuse and global radiation (if not during the dark of winter) are recorded and reported to NIWA's meteorological division back in New Zealand. This study is one of the longest continuous records in Antarctica, with observations having been made since 1957.

A measure of precipitation is made once each year using a special rain gauge. A layer of kerosene floats on any water collected to prevent evaporation.

Event K102: Seismology

Two systems are in operation to measure earthquake activity. The older WWSS (World Wide Seismic System) is fully manual with four helicorders measuring various components of earthquake wave propagation. The data are collected from detectors in the earth outside Scott Base an recorded on helicorder charts. Preliminary results are reported to an international seismology centre in the United States and a final analysis of the charts is made at the Institute of Geological and Nuclear Science (IGNS) in Wellington.

The second system is fully automated with data telemetred from detectors near Vanda Station to Scott base, then on to Albuquerque in the United States. This system is run by the United States Geological Survey with the co-operation of New Zealand's IGNS.

These systems in relatively 'seismically quiet' Antarctica can measure major earthquakes from all over the world. The WWSS operation has continued since IGY.

Event K103: Geomagnetics

The strength and direction of the earth's magnetic field are recorded by an automated system of continuous measurement and a set of weekly manual readings is made for calibration purposes. These data are sent on to IGNS in New Zealand. Scott Base has a unique location for making such measurements as it is almost halfway between the earth's geographic and magnetic south poles. This recording has continued since IGY.

Event K104: Ionospherics

A transmitter sends a series of varying radio frequency waves skyward and a receiver picks up reflected pulses off the ionosphere (the zone of ionisation starting 60km above the earth's surface). This produces data that are presented as an 'ionogram', which portrays the ionisation state of the ionosphere. IGNS processes this data.

Sunspot activity, which disrupts ionisation, shows up as no ionogram pattern. In the days of HF radio communication this could mean no communication, as these waves need an ionosphere to bounce off. Today's satellite communications do not rely on the integrity of the ionosphere.

Appendix Two

SCOTT BASE METEOROLOGICAL RECORD 1994-95 SEASON

Month	Temperature (°C)				Wind (knots)
	Mean	(1957–92 Mean*)	Max	Min	Max Gust
October '94	-19.4	(-22.0)	-4.0	-36.4	57
November	-11.4	(-11.2)	-3.0	-21.0	60
December	-5.1	(-5.0)	+2.0	-19.2	32
January '95	-5.5	(-4.7)	+1.6	-15.6	30
February	-11.1	(-11.1)	+1.3	-24.4	54
March	-22.9	(-20.2)	-9.8	-40.3	59
April	-28.2	(-24.0)	-10.9	-44.6	43
May	-29.4	(-26.2)	-10.2	-49.6	69
June	-26.3	(-26.3)	-8.2	-46.2	67
July	-29.2	(-29.1)	-14.1	-44.0	46
August	-28.3	(-30.2)	-7.8	-44.8	56
September	-28.2	(-28.1)	-10.3	-48.7	63

NB: Apart from October 1994 and August 1995 the 1994-95 monthly means are the same as or less than the 1957-92 means.

* From NIWA's *The Climate of Scott Base* 1957-92 by A.M. (Tony) Bromley.

Appendix Three

Scott Base Support & Event Staff 1994-95

BASE STAFF
Base Management

Dave Geddes	Senzrep (Oct-Dec)
Malcolm Macfarlane	Senzrep (Dec-Feb)
Alan Wilson	Operations support manager
Graham White	Base services manager

Winter-Over Staff

Bruce Calder	Electrician
Dave Mitchell	Base engineer
Jan Stratford	Domestic
Jim McKenzie	Telecom technician
Joe Ford	Mechanic
John Williams	Engineering services manager
	Deputy winter manager
Sean Flanagan	Science technician
Shane Scott	Chef
Tom Hopkins	Field support officer
Warren Herrick	Base support officer
	Winter manager

Summer Support Staff

Shane Atkins	Plant operator
Ang Tutua	Communications operator
Ava Nathan	Domestic
Bevan Gerling	Supply officer
Dan Keller	Carpenter
Dennis Ham	Mechanic
Gary Smith	Carpenter
Gloria Mooney	Communications operator
Jacqui Steele	Domestic
Jo Kilpatrick	Postal/admin clerk
Lynette Simmonds	Senior communications officer
Mat Mataroa	Cargo handler
Scott Taylor	Chef
Shaun Smith	Canteen manager
Steve Thomas	Science technician
Lindsay Taylor	Plant operator

FIELD SUPPORT STAFF

Cullum Boleyn	Vanda carpenter
Rachel Brown	AFT instructor
Tarn Pilkington	AFT instructor
Warren Herrick	AFT leader

SCIENCE EVENT STAFF

Listed in Appendix One

OTHER EVENT STAFF
Antarctic Heritage Trust

John Charles
Lawrence Smith

Neville Ritchie
Roger Fyfe

DOSLI (Survey) Assistance

Perry Gilbert

ICAIR Visitors

Dawn-Lee Hartley
Dean Ashby

Media

Aaron Devitt	TVNZ
Alan Henderson	TVNZ
Mike Rehu	TVNZ
Paul Skelton	TVNZ
Jo Andrews	ITN
Peter Wilkinson	ITN
Keith Lyons	Freelance

Operation White Safari

John Crighton	Navy	Richard Tawhiri	Army
Brent Snopovs	Navy	Jude Anker	Army
Graeme Hearn	Navy	Michelle de Vries	Army
Lisa Glennie	Navy	Reuben Merrett	Army

Telecom Maintenance

Bryce Kerr
Chris Robertson
Dean Flintoft
Jim McGregor

Youth Group Visitors

Colin Robcke
Glenda Walker

RNZAF 3 (Iroquois) Squadron

(Based at McMurdo)

Flight crew (Nov)	*Ground crew (Nov-Dec)*
Rangi Pirihi	Richard Stent
Keith Buckley	Grant Plested
Darren Goodwin	Peter Burke
	Peter Wilson
Flight crew (Dec)	Zak Edmonds
Tim Donaldson	
Stu Blair	
Hek Heke	*Ground crew (Jan)*
	John Bartlett
Flight crew (Jan)	Grant Bennie
Paul Stockley	Jacko Jackson
Stu Brownlie	Mel McGrath
Ty Cochran	Rex McCowatt

Appendix Four

McMurdo Winter-over Staff 1995

MANAGEMENT

Al Martin	NSF McMurdo winter manager
Karen Schwall	ASA manager
Scott Humpert	NSFA officer in charge

NSFA
Administration

Bill Auchincloss	Admin officer
Les Brown	Admin yeoman
Glen McPhail	Billetting
Marvin Tucker	Personnel officer
Geoff DeVore	Disbursing officer

Medical

Dr Randy Hyer	Medical officer
Tom Dagostino	Senior medical corpsman
Tony Miller	Medical corpsman
Tony Zilar	Medical corpsman

Morale, Welfare & Recreation

Rod Withers	Director
Brendan McKendry	Assistant
Nell Boche	Assistant
Raymond Smith	Assistant

Operations

Tony Lopinto	Operations officer
Kim Hall	Air traffic control
Bernard Sanchez	Computer technician
Ty Rolle	Electronics Division officer
Christine Smock	Electronics technician
David Navas	Electronics technician
Mark Chambers	Electronics technician
Scott Schroeder	Electronics technician
Eva Vanmiddlesworth	Radio Division officer
Cynthia Thompson	Radio operator
Ken Grant	Radio operator
Sean Shulander	Radio operator
Joe Spain	Weather forecaster
Angie Gardiner	Weather observer
Rick Mendoza	Weather observer

ASA
Administration

Val Carroll	Co-ordinator
Shelley Kuder	Quality control

Facilities Maintenance

Ralph Stokes	FMC manager

MalBritt Bennett	Administrator
Pami Morin	Administrator
David Khoo	Work order planner
Gary Teestell	Crary Lab maintenance engineer
John Sale	Field engineering surveyor
Tom Moody	Field engineering surveyor
Bobby Lozano	Draftsman
Randy Olsen	Construction co-ordinator
J.B. Freeman	Construction co-ordinator
Jim McCarton	Preventative maintenance foreman
Howard Smith	Boiler mechanic
Patrick Able	Boiler mechanic
Steve Bertola	Boiler mechanic
Tony Machetti	Carpenter
Mike Trboyevich	Carpenter
Jay Foraker	Carpenter
Joe Bennett	Carpenter
Russell McLean	Carpenter
Thom Miller	Carpenter
Todd Brown	Carpenter
Donald Poehler	Electrician
Bob Foley	Electrician
Daniel Nielsen	Electrician
Donald Epps	Electrician
Michael Baker	Electrician
Paul Belarde	Electrician
Scott Tomczyk	Electrician
Tim Hoog	Electrician
William Almy	Electrician
Andrew Prchlik	Fire protection
Jeffrey Koerschen	Fire protection
Alan Hogan	General assistant
Heather Haugland	General assistant
Niam Moody	General assistant
Robert Kaul	General assistant
Richard Perales	Insulator
Kris Turnbull	Lineman
Steen Elschens	Lineman
Vincent Putras	Lineman
Brad Kuehn	Metalworker
Bobby Drake	Metalworker
David DelMastro	Painter
Joseph Milligan	Painter
Michelle Hartford	Painter
Leroy Dunsworth	Plumber
David Breining	Plumber
Frank Maddy	Plumber
Harold Gober	Plumber
John Crenshaw	Plumber
Mark Wilson	Plumber
Paul Bjorkman	Plumber
Scott Smith	Plumber

Trenton Prochko	Plumber
Michael Blachut	Refrigeration mechanic
Dave Martin	Utility mechanic
Jon McIntyre	Utility mechanic
Madison Hall	Utility mechanic
Richard Segler	Utility mechanic

Food Services

Tom Carver	Food services manager
Trine Gjorstad	Baker
Chris Erb	Cook
Esther Boone	Cook
Glenn Rooth	Cook
Lenore Hinson	Cook
Lester Bracy	Cook
Marci Tackett	Cook
Peggy Ann Rogers	Cook
Dean Shapiro	Dining room attendant
Erik Larson	Dining room attendant
Judy Stacy	Dining room attendant
Michelle Shaefer	Dining room attendant
Roren Stowell	Dining room attendant
Vicki Howarth	Dining room attendant

Housing

Hope Stout	Housing manager
Melanie Strom	Hair stylist/laundry
Alan Wood	Janitor
Andrea White	Janitor
Andrea Winkler	Janitor
Christy Parrott	Janitor
Daire Ochs	Janitor
Sue Navas	Janitor
Tom Fliss	Janitor

Informations Systems

Jeff Smith	Infosys manager
Tonya DeCroce	Administrator
Yvonne Ramager	Administrator
Jill Labelle	Work order planner
Andrew Crowley	Help desk
Al Oxton	Communications technician
Mitch Perry	Communications technician
Bob Rehmel	Communications technician
Kevin Neighbours	Communications technician
Jeffri Frontz	Computer technician
Ethan Dicks	Computer technician
Bob Palko	Computer field engineer
Michael Hancock	Mapcon programmer
Jon Taulbee	Telephone technician

Logistics

Betsy Hoagland	Logistics manager
Rebecca Simonson	Clerk
Steve Kraemer	Mapcon data specialist
Jennifer Moxon	Inventory controller
Juan Reyes	Inventory controller
Marilyn Younger	Inventory controller
Eileen Tams	Requisition controller
James Fortson	Central supply
Alberto Jurado	Central supply
Robert Callahan	Central supply
Vern Pomraning	Construction

Bill Bennett	Construction
Bill Ruddell	Construction
Craig Dunne	Construction
Woody Porter	Crary Lab
Diane Wetterlin	Crary Lab
Lisa Williams	Crary Lab
Mariah Crossland	Electrical
Duane Stark	Electrical
Dave Starling	Electronics
Rafael Pizano	Food services
Jeff Cowman	Food services
Connie Nottke	Heavy vehicle maintenance
Barb Propst	Heavy vehicle maintenance
Dave Murry	Heavy vehicle maintenance
Deb Walton	Heavy vehicle maintenance
Gina Williams	Heavy vehicle maintenance
Mike Minneci	Heavy vehicle maintenance
Scott Enlow	Heavy vehicle maintenance
Sunny Brock	Heavy vehicle maintenance
Carol Gould	Materials
Catherine Nelson	Materials
Cheryl Gulick	Materials
Mark Lopus	Materials
Sharon Stacey	Materials
Sandy Grandchamp	Mechanical equipment
Ken Narvarro	Plumbing/utility/metals
Ben Koontz	Plumbing/utility/metals
Jennifer Starling	Plumbing/utility/metals
John White	Plumbing/utility/metals
Mike Birkmeyer	Power and water

Operations

Rocky Ness	Operations manager
Jennifer Carter	Administration
Sam Williams	Equipment operations foreman
Dan Aldous	Equipment operator
Don Stacey	Equipment operator
James Mickelson	Equipment operator
Jim Parr	Equipment operator
Larry Strow	Equipment operator
Rex Cortner	Equipment operator
Sundown Semmler	Equipment operator
Ron Hendricks	Fuels
Larry Brown	Fuels
John Rasor	Power and water supervisor
Chris Moxon	Power and water mechanic
Christopher Herring	Power and water mechanic
James Day	Power and water mechanic
Johnny Cofield	Power and water mechanic
Ron O'Brien	Power and water mechanic
Allen Beggren	Power and water technician
Andy Testin	Power and water technician
Dan Smith	Power and water technician
Dave Smith	Power and water technician
David Evensen	Power and water technician
Lyle Zinke	Power and water technician
Robert Simpson	Power and water technician
Wendy Kober	Power and water technician
John Bostick	Vehicle maintenance supervisor
Mary Hunter	Administration
Bill Layman	Mechanic
Dan Robinson	Mechanic
Dave Selzler	Mechanic
Diamond Western	Mechanic

Ed Matilla	Mechanic
Ed Stockard	Mechanic
Harry Egeland	Mechanic
James Lester	Mechanic
James Murphy	Mechanic
Kevin Steichen	Mechanic
Louis Birkmeyer	Mechanic
Russ Poorman	Mechanic
Steve Hagel	Mechanic
Bob Sheld	Machinist
Terry Trimingham	Workshop assistant

Science Support

Tim Cully	Science support & BFC manager
Gail Noton	Crary Lab supervisor
Joe Longo	Science technician
Beth Sheld	Science facility technician
Kari Noring	BFC technician
Marcello DelGiudice	Toboggan mechanic
Malvin Martin	Field equipment mechanic

Safety & Environmental Health

Steve Drummond	Fire Dept captain
Barb Martin	Dispatcher

Ron Ramirez	Fire inspector
Chad Schneider	Fire crew
Chris Jung	Fire crew
Corky Self	Fire crew
Fritz Snyder	Fire crew
Jeff Akens	Fire crew
Jeff Pickering	Fire crew
Mark Melton	Fire crew
Mike Chappell	Fire crew
Scott Howard	Fire crew
Tobi Anderson	Fire crew
Tom Vinson	Haz-waste supervisor
Rudi Kirse	Haz-waste technician
Cindy Root	Solid waste supervisor
Che Gilland	Waste management technician
Chris Teske	Waste management technician
Doug Fink	Waste management technician
Shelly Weston	Waste management technician
Jeff Ryan	Waste equipment operator

NSF SCIENTISTS

Don Slack	Radar satellite facility
Tom Pennel	Radar satellite facility

Appendix Five

Scott Base (& Vanda) Winter-over Teams

1956–57
Edmund Hillary	Leader
Bob Miller	Deputy leader
George Marsh	Doctor
Trevor Hatherton	Scientific leader
Vern Gerard	Physicist
Herb Orr	Technical officer
Neil Sandford	Technical officer
Peter MacDonald	Technical officer
Bernie Gunn	Geologist
Guy Warren	Geologist
Ron Balham	Zoologist
Selwyn Bucknell	Cook
Murray Ellis	Engineer
Jim Bates	Mechanic
Harry Ayers	Field leader/dog handler
Murray Douglas	Field/dog handler
Richard Brooke	Surveyor
Roy Carlyon	Surveyor
Ted Gawn	Radio
Peter Mulgrew	Radio technician
John Claydon	RNZAF pilot
Bill Cranfield	RNZAF pilot
Wally Tarr	RNZAF mechanic

1957-58
Lin Martin	Leader
Don Thompson	Senior scientist
Bob Henderson	Technician
Buzz Burrows	Technician
Franco Faggioni	Scientist (Italy)
Graeme Midwinter	Scientist
Maurice Speary	Cook
Murray Robb	Diesel engineer
Les Duff	Mechanic
Peter Yeates	Radio officer
Mike Gibson	Radio technician

1958-59
Rod Hewitt	Leader
Brian Sandford	Senior scientist
Mervyn Rodgers	Technician
Al Stuart	Scientist (US)
Frans van der Hoeven	Scientist (US)
Paul Heiser	Scientist (US)
Eric Wedgewood	Cook
Graham Ward	Senior maintenance officer
Leonard Sales	Maintenance officer
Arnold Heine	Stores/NZGSE
Ken Wise	Field/NZGSE
Peter Phillips	Radio operator
Ron Pemberton	Radio technician

1959-60
James Lennox-King	Leader
Colin Bailey	Medical officer
Frank McNeil	Senior scientist
Don Webster	Science technician
Colin Jenness	Technician
Dudley Holmes	Technician
Jack Taylor	Technician
John Warren	Cook
Robert Buckley	Maintenance officer
Graeme Johnstone	Mechanic
Robert Collins	Carpenter
Garth Matterson	Surveyor
Peter Hunt	Surveyor
Peter Yeates	Radio officer

1960-61
Mick Donnelly	Leader
Bob Clements	Senior scientist
Bob Cranfield	Technician
Peter Graham	Technician
Uwe Sobiecki	Technician
Rory Shanahan	Scientist
Ken Fairclough	Cook
Ray Logie	Senior maintenance officer
Bernard Foley	Maintenance officer
Bill Hare	Mechanic
Wally Herbert	Field/NZGSE
Peter Otway	Surveyor/NZGSE
Bill Deverall	Radio officer

1961-62
Athol Roberts	Leader
Ian Richards	Senior scientist
Alexander French	Technician
Anthony Langston	Technician
Grant Williams	Technician
Caleb Beech	Cook
John Mills	Senior maintenance officer
Bill Timms	Electrician
Graham McKenty	Carpenter
Kevin Pain	Field assistant/NZGSE
Ronald Hewson	Surveyor/NZGSE
Howard O'Kane	Photographer
Eric Vickers	Radio operator

1962-63
Ronald Tinker	Leader
George Lewis	Senior scientist
Ian Cave	Scientific officer
Don Webster	Technician
Trevor Ancell	Technician

Murray Smith	Biologist
Les Wells	Cook
Bill Doull	Electrician
Leonard Louden	Mechanic
Barry Waters	Carpenter
James Graveson	Field assistant/driller
Maurice Sheehan	Field assistant
Malcolm Ford	Surveyor/NZGSE
Quentin McLea	Radio officer

1963-64
Russell Rawle	Leader
George Lewis	Senior scientist
Duncan Miller	Scientific officer
Hereward Horsfield	Technician
Thomas Hetherington	Technician
Bryan George	Chef
Bill Lucy	Surveyor/handyman
John Mills	Base engineer
John Fabian	Fitter/mechanic
Brian Judd	Fitter/electrician
Gerald Graham	Carpenter
Dave Massam	Handyman/field assistant
Ted Gawn	Radio operator

1964-65
Adrian Hayter	Leader
Buzz Burrows	Senior scientist
George Jones	Technician
Jack Calvert	Technician
Trevor Sanson	Technician
Yogi Foster-Lynam	Technician
John Haycock	Cook
Brian Judd	Base engineer
Brian Dorrington	Electrician
Charlie Hough	Mechanic
Dave Lowe	Field assistant
Ivan McDonald	Field assistant
Bob Wright	Stores
Ted Gawn	Radio operator

1965-66
Michael Prebble	Leader
Andrew Porter	Senior scientist
Ian Johnson	Senior technician
David Randell	Technician
Ray Vickers	Technician
Aivin Davidson	Cook
Norman Dewson	Base engineer
Allan Junge	Electrician
Terence McGeough	Mechanic
Raynor Greeks	Carpenter
Roger Bartlett	Field assistant
Gerard Ternahan	Radio operator

1966-67
Colin Clark	Leader
Gordon Dawson	Senior technical officer
Peter Whiteford	Scientific officer
Bob Murdoch	Technician
Warwick Earl	Technician
Bryan George	Cook
Chris Rickards	Electrician
Bob Sopp	Diesel mechanic

Robin Kidd	Vehicle mechanic
Bob Rae	AMO
Warwick Orchiston	Field assistant/dogs
Norm White	Radio officer

1967-68
Bill Webb	Leader
Ian Johnson	Senior science technician
Dave Henderson	Technician
John Talbot	Technician
Warwick Fergusson	Technician
Ian Wratt	Cook
Russell Houliston	Electrician
Carey Irwin	Vehicle mechanic
Alan Magee	Diesel mechanic
Grahame Champness	Field assistant/dogs
George Edlin	Postmaster

1968-69
Robin Foubister	Leader
Peter Lennard	Senior technical officer
Keith Mandeno	Technician
Nigel Millar	Technician
Geoff Gill	Cook
Allan Guard	Base engineer
Chris Rickards	Electrician
Wayne Maguiness	Mechanic
Noel Wilson	Field assistant/dogs
Brian Hool	Postmaster
David Blackbourn	PO radio technician

Vanda
Bill Lucy	Leader
Simon Cutfield	Scientific officer
Ron Craig	Met observer
Warren Johns	Technician
Allan Riordan	Scientist (US)

1969-70
Bruce Willis	Leader
Peter Graham	Senior technician
Peter Hide	Technician
Peter Kerr	Technician
Russell Powick	Chef
Howard Marriott	Base engineer
Peter Wigg	Fitter electrician
Roger Lusby	Fitter mechanic
Chris Knott	Field assistant
Bob Hancock	Postmaster
Ian Wilton	PO radio technician

Vanda
Harold Lowe	Leader
Gary Lewis	Senior technical officer
Tony Bromley	Meteorologist
Bob McKerrow	Technician

1970-71
Brian Porter	Leader
Ron Nimmo	Senior technical officer
David Clough	Technician
Murray Dawson	Technician
Jim Rankin	Base engineer
Frank Bond	Cook

Alec McFerran	Electrician
Stuart Millar	Mechanic
Paul Christensen	AMO
Mac Riding	Field assistant/dogs
Graham Crooks	Postmaster
Jim Windsor	Radio technician

1971-72
Jim Barker	Leader
John Elder	Scientific officer
John Maine	Technician
Kevin Weatherall	Technician
Peter McNeill	Chef
Malcolm MacDonald	Base engineer
David Clark	Electrician
Roger Parkinson	AMO/mechanic
Dick McBride	PRO/field assistant
Allan Burgess	Postmaster
Kevin Matson	Radio technician

1972-73
Peter Frazer	Leader
Phil Owens	Senior technician
John Williams	Technician
Philip Scothern	Technician
John Halewood	Chef
John Housiaux	Base engineer
Wayne Reeves	Electrician
George Turner	Mechanic
John Bitters	AMO/dogs
Neville Copeland	Postmaster
Allan Dawrant	PO radio technician

1973-74
Harry Jones	OIC
Tony Atkinson	Senior technical officer
Garth Cowan	Technician
Stuart Clarke	Technician
Ray Colliver	Cook
Bill Johnston	Base engineer
Chris Wilkins	Electrician
Bob Grant	Mechanic
Mike Wing	Field assistant/dogs
Titch Gibson	Postmaster
Les Walker	PO radio technician

Vanda
Tony Bromley	Leader/meteorologist
Tony Smith	Technician
Peter Thompson	Technician
Bob Newlands	AMO

1974-75
Jim Newman	OIC
Dave Hope	Technician
Craig Nickerson	Technician
Peter Jemmett	Technician
Ken Parker	Cook
Garry McCullough	Base engineer
Bob Kitchener	Electrician
Robert Livingstone	Mechanic
John Stevens	AMO/dogs
Alan Campbell	Postmaster
Allan Hardie	PO radio technician

1975-76
Hamish Raynham	OIC
Roger Jones	Senior technician
Chris Mills	Technician
Clint Davis	Technician
Ian MacLeod	Cook
Ted Ramsbotham	Base engineer
John Thomson	Fitter mechanic
Grant Eames	AMO/mechanic
Mike Wing	Field assistant/dogs
Barry Scannell	Postmaster
Allan Dawrant	PO radio technician

1976-77
Jim Rankin	OIC/base engineer
Kevin Weatherall	Senior technical officer
Ian Minchington	Technician
Rod Fearn	Technician
Roel Keizer	Chef
Ian Booker	Fitter mechanic
Howard Richards	Fitter electrician
Richard Wills	Field assistant/dogs
Ian Johnstone	Postmaster
George Money	PO radio technician

1977-78
John Lythgoe	OIC
Warwick Williams	Senior technical officer
Dean Drake	Technician
Will Kimber	Technician
Russell Arnott	Chef
John Thomson	Base engineer
Mike Lord	Fitter electrician
Barry Hiscock	Fitter mechanic
Steve Chambers	Dog handler
Randy Waller	Postmaster
Paul Dennison	PO radio technician

1978-79
John Presland	OIC
Thelma Rodgers	Scientific officer
Alan Burt	Technician
Ray Vincent	Technician
Brent Trevathan	Chef
Tom Stephenson	Base engineer
Chris Cunningham	Fitter electrician
Bob Geddes	Fitter mechanic
Graeme Abernathy	AMO
Peter Cleary	Field assistant/dogs
Maurice Challinor	Postmaster
Allister Babington	PO radio technician

1979-80
Cas Roper	OIC/senior technical officer
Dave Rees	DOIC/AMO
Roger Phillips	Technician
Warwick Bull	Chef
Norm Hills	Base engineer
Rex Hendry	Electrician
Brian Hagan	Mechanic
Con Faber	Field assistant/dogs
Doug Keown	Storekeeper
Leo Slattery	Postmaster
Andy Hayden	PO radio technician

1980-81

John Sims	OIC/base engineer
Tom Earl	DOIC/senior technical officer
Don McKnight	Scientific officer
Stan Whitfield	Technician
Allan Remnant	Chef
John Mackey	Electrician
Bruce Scott	Mechanic
Allan Taylor	Field assistant/dogs
Ian Johnstone	Postmaster
Robin Hodgson	PO radio technician

1981-82

Leo Slattery	OIC/postmaster
Keith Martin	DOIC/base engineer
Chris Choros	Senior technical officer
Peter Wheeler	Technician
Ross Mason	Technician
Graeme Morgan	Chef
Rick Walshe	Electrician
Peter Nelson	Mechanic
Gary Bowcock	Field assistant/dogs
Allister Babington	PO technician

1982-83

Graham Woodhead	OIC
Rex Johnson	DOIC/PO radio technician
Andrew Harrall	Technician
Doug Martin	Technician
Gary Brown	Technician
Chris Kelly	Chef
Lew Pemberton	Base engineer
Norm Wear	Electrician
Kerry Kirkness	Mechanic
Bill Eaton	Field assistant/dogs
Steve Johnson	Postmaster

1983-84

Eric Saxby	OIC
Ian Sayers	DOIC/postmaster
Ralph Holwerda	Senior technician
Chris Fry	Technician
Jeremy Ireland	Technician
Ian McDonald	Chef
Rod Vardy	Base engineer
Brian Hobern	Electrician
John Hoffman	Mechanic
Al Roy	Field assistant/dogs
Murray Kennett	PO technician

1984-85

Leo Slattery	OIC/postmaster
Tony Grant	Senior technician
Brian Lawson	Technician
Peter Turner	Technician
George Moir	Chef
Dennis Shaw	Base engineer
Owen Taylor	Electrician
Peter Nelson	Mechanic
Jock Walton	Carpenter
Kevin Conaglen	Field assistant/dogs
Keith Graham	PO technician

1985-86

Jim Rankin	OIC/base engineer
Steve Loney	DOIC/postmaster
Mike Harman	Senior scientific officer
Don Wilkinson	Technician
Ross Paterson	Technician
Greg Crocker	Scientist (BAS)
Steve Mosley	Chef
Ross McDonald	Assistant base engineer
Steve Pardoe	Electrician
Barry Hiscock	Mechanic
Richard Balm	Field assistant/dogs
Paul Purves	PO technician

1986-87

Keith Martin	OIC/base engineer
Nick Miller	Senior scientific officer
Dave Stevens	Technician
Paul Denyer	Technician
Kerry Paterson	Chef
Steve Orr	Assistant base engineer
Brett Whitley	Electrician
Bill Ratahi	Mechanic
Dave Brice	Field/stores
Gavin Sanne	Postmaster
John O'Donoghue	PO technician

1987-88

Malcolm Macfarlane	OIC/senior scientific officer
Terry Ashdown	DOIC/engineering manager
Dave Barrett	Technician
Stan Whitfield	Technician
Brendan Davis	Chef
Wendy Trail	General duties
Bob Geddes	Base engineer
John Thorpe	Mechanic
Al Fastier	Electrician
Paul Wilson	Field/stores
Alan Meek	Comms supervisor
Paul Purves	Telecom technician

1988-89

Nigel Millar	OIC/senior technical officer
Howard Nicholson	Technician
Tim Exley	Technician
Kerry Paterson	Chef
Biddy Harnett	General duties
Brian Howell	Engineering manager
Terry Eason	Base engineer
Graham Hickey	Electrician
Sean Heaphy	Mechanic
Dave Brice	Field/stores
Heather Gilmore	Comms supervisor
Matt Arthur	Telecom technician

1989-90

Alister Pringle	OIC/comms supervisor
Alistair Gillespie	Senior technician
Bruce McGregor	Technician
Wendy Strid	Chef
Tuppence Loe	General duties
Duncan Webb	Engineering manager
Tony Oskram	Base engineer
Bruce Calder	Electrician

Peter Nelson — Mechanic
Doug Henderson — Field/stores
Dave Robertson — Telecom technician

1990-91
Ross McDonald — Base manager/engineering manager
Chris McCarroll — Technician
Peter Kraak — Technician
Karen Gage — Chef
Sally White — Domestic
Peter Harding — Base engineer (until June Medivac)
Bob Geddes — Base engineer (following Medivac)
Max Olliver — Electrician
Jack Jenniskens — Mechanic
Phil Clerke — Field/stores
Helen Wills — Telecom operator
Roy Joblin — Telecom technician
Max Quinn — TVNZ producer/director
Don Anderson — TVNZ sound recordist

1991-92
Kerry Paterson — Base manager/chef
Grant Avery — Technician
Therese Dobbs — Domestic
Shane Coleman — Engineering manager
Brian Howat — Base engineer
Brett Whitley — Electrician
Mike Collins — Mechanic
Jim Henderson — Field/stores
Bella Kara — Telecom supervisor
Paul Purves — Telecom technician

1992-93
Roger Moffat — Base manager/engineering manager
Mike Mahon — Technician
Cath George — Chef (until Winfly)
Shane Scott — Chef (Winfly)
Viv Taylor — Domestic
Andy Goodall — Base engineer
Brian Green — Electrician (until Winfly)
Brian Reid — Electrician (Winfly)
Greg Harris — Mechanic
Rob Johnston — Base assistant

Dave Brice — Field/stores
Callum McGowan — Telecom technician

1993-94
Grant Avery — Winter manager/science technician
Steve Wood — Ozone scientist
Art Bosman — Chef
Ange Bocock — Domestic
Dave Lucas — Engineering services manager
Dom McCarthy — Base engineer
Grant West — Electrician
Jeremy Ridgen — Mechanic
Belinda Bennett — Base support officer
Bruce Janes — Field support officer
Eric Trip — Telecom technician

1994-95
Warren Herrick — Winter manager/ base support officer
John Williams — Deputy winter manager/ engineering services manager
Sean Flanagan — Science technician
Shane Scott — Chef
Jan Stratford — Domestic
Dave Mitchell — Base engineer
Bruce Calder — Electrician
Joe Ford — Mechanic
Tom Hopkins — Field support officer
Jim McKenzie — Telecom technician

1995/96
Ron Rogers — Winter manager/ engineering services manager
Stewart Hopkins — Deputy winter manager/chef
David Hornstein — Science technician
Alana Muir — Domestic
Steve Harry — Base engineer
Steven Palmer — Base engineer
Mike Pahl — Electrician
Robyn Holland — Base support officer
Jim Henderson — Field support officer
Eric Trip — Telecom technician

GLOSSARY

AFCC	Armed Forces Canteen Council
AFT	Antarctic Field Training
AHT	Antarctic Heritage Trust
AMO	Assistant maintenance officer
ASA	Antarctic Support Associates
BA	Breathing apparatus
bag drag	Baggage check-in at McMurdo
BAS	British Antarctic Survey
beaker	Colloquialism for scientist
BFC	Berg Field Centre (at McMurdo)
boondoggle	American equivalent of 'fam'
BSM	Base services manager
comms	Radio communications
DNF	Do not freeze
DSIR	Department of Scientific and Industrial Research
DV	Distinguished visitor
EGT	Erebus Glacier Tongue
ESM	Engineering services manager
ETA	Estimated time of arrival
event	The term used for a mission on ice, whether for the purposes of science, publicity, a works programme or historic site preservation. Each event is designated numerically (eg Kiwi 001 or K001)
fam	Recreational 'familiarisation' trip away from base
fast ice	Areas of the sea ice sheet that are fixed into position, particularly near the coastline and between headlands
freshies	Fresh fruit and vegetables
GD	General duties
GPS	Global positioning system
Helo Ops	Helicopter Operations
herbie	Storm with strong wind and blowing snow
Herc	C-130 or LC-130 (ski-equipped) Hercules
HF	High frequency
IGNS	Institute of Geological and Nuclear Science
IGY	International Geophysical Year (1957-58)
ITN	Independent Television News
JASART	Joint Antarctic Search and Rescue Team
JP-8	Aircraft turbine fuel with additives
Mac Ops	McMurdo Operations – McMurdo's NSFA communications and air operations facility

Met obs	Meteorological observations
mouse round	Rostered evening inspection of base
mukluk	A heavy-duty Japanese insulated boot (an Inuit word)
MWR	Morale, welfare and recreation (McMurdo)
NIWA	National Institute of Water and Atmospheric Research
NGO	Non-governmental organisation
NSF	National Science Foundation (US)
NSFA	Naval Support Force Antarctica
NZAP	New Zealand Antarctic Programme
NZGSE	New Zealand Geological Survey Expedition
OIC	Officer in charge
OSM	Operations support manager
PA	Public address paging system
prussik	A climbing technique using two light loops of cord, tied to a rope with prussik knots, to ascend a vertical rope
PSR	Point of safe return
RDF	Radio direction finder
RDRC	Ross Dependency Research Committee
RNZAF	Royal New Zealand Air Force
RO	Reverse osmosis
salopettes	Bib-style pants
SAR	Search and rescue
sastrugi	Irregular ridges of wind-toughened snow
Senzrep	Senior New Zealand representative
SES	Satellite Earth Station
Sorrels	Canadian brand of cold-weather insulated boots
SSSI	Site of Special Scientific Interest
TAE	Trans-Antarctic Expedition
transition	Zone where the sea ice meets land or ice shelf
USAP	United States Antarctic Programme
USGS	United States Geological Survey
VHF	Very high frequency
Winfly	The period from the end of winter (when the sun returns) until the start of summer. A number of LC-130 flights are made at the beginning of Winfly.
whiteout	When uniformly overcast conditions over a snow-covered surface prevent any surface or horizon being defined.
WWSS	World-wide Seismic System